THE STRUCTURE OF
JULIUS CAESAR

THE STRUCTURE OF

JULIUS CAESAR

by

ADRIEN BONJOUR

Professor of English
in the University of Neuchâtel

LIVERPOOL UNIVERSITY PRESS
1958

Published by

LIVERPOOL UNIVERSITY PRESS

123 Grove Street · Liverpool 7

First Published 1958

PRINTED IN GREAT BRITAIN BY EATON PRESS AT LIVERPOOL

To Professor G. Bonnard

LAREOWA SELEST ON ÐÆM DÆGE ÐISSES LIFES

By the Same Author

Coleridge's 'Hymn Before Sunrise'.
>   A Study of Facts and Problems Connected with the Poem.
>   La Concorde, Lausanne. 1942.

Dialogue de Saint-Julien et son Disciple : Poème Anglo-Normand du XIIIe Siècle.
>   Anglo-Norman Texts VIII. Blackwell, Oxford. 1949.

The Digressions in 'Beowulf'.
>   Medium Ævum Monographs V. Blackwell, Oxford. 1950.

ACKNOWLEDGMENTS

Spiritually, this little book is a testimony of the dangers of indulgent criticism on the part of some Shakespearean scholars. This proved enough of an incentive to urge me to lapse into print and, worse still, this urge could hardly be stopped short of perpetrating a book. That it is small is at least an extenuating circumstance, if not a saving clause, and this is partly due to the fact that the subject lent itself to a treatment in the form of lectures rather than an elaborate treatise in the manner of certain *bahnbrechende Forscher*. In any case, even a book is but another ripple in the multitudinous seas of Shakespearean criticism, soon merged into the general current, lost into the infinite expanse, and gone with the trade-wind.

Materially, it is the result of a generous grant from the Swiss National Fund for Scientific Research, which made possible a stay at the Shakespeare Institute of Stratford, where the book was written in 1953 (at a time when the drudgery of teaching duties of the most elementary kind would otherwise have prevented any research work). Substantial, and most welcome, contributions towards the publication of the book were generously granted by the "Société Académique Vaudoise" and the University of Lausanne.

It has become an orthodox and commendable rite for those involved in Shakespeare to bow to their countless predecessors—with, or without, the ceremonial shot of a Parthian arrow. And I follow it (I mean the rite) all the more devotedly since I somehow feel like the Burgundian snail who, be it remembered, was able to reach Dijon—no mean achievement for an eminently pedestrian gasteropod—because he was carried on the brush of the fast-footed Fox, and then succeeded in climbing the gate which halted crafty master Reynard. A good thing, at least, for the pedestrian critic that once he has climbed the wall to peep into the garden of Shakespeare's art, he runs lesser risks than the nimble-footed one of suddenly finding the " humtyhillhead of humself in quest of his humtytumtoes."

Individually, my thanks are first due to my master, Professor G. Bonnard, whose active and stimulating interest in my own researches made this study possible. My gratitude also goes to Professor Allardyce Nicoll, who allowed me to make liberal use of the fine library of the Shakespeare Institute, and to Mr. R. A.

Foakes, who patiently acted there as my indispensable cicerone. Mr. J. G. O'Kane, of the Liverpool University Press, kindly gave most useful advice on all matters pertaining to the printing of the study. The greatest debt, however, I owe to Professor Kenneth Muir, who accepted the time-consuming and unrewarding task of acting as a godfather to the study—which was particularly generous, since his own publications are steadily growing (as every scholar concerned in English Literature knows) into a more and more impressive family.

ADRIEN BONJOUR

Vevey, October 1957.

PREFACE

Although *Julius Caesar* appears to be one of the least complex of Shakespeare's plays, so that on one level it can be appreciated by schoolboys, it has evoked a number of conflicting interpretations. Some have regarded Brutus as one of freedom's martyrs, and others would place him in the lowest circle of hell. To some critics the play has seemed to be lacking in unity, the centre of interest changing from one act to the next. Brutus has been condemned as a failure of portraiture because of Shakespeare's lack of interest in republicanism. In recent years, however, a number of critics have contributed to our understanding of the play. Mr. G. Wilson Knight has characteristically analysed some of its themes ; Mr. John Palmer has made a study of its political characters ; Professor L. C. Knights has written brilliantly on Shakespeare's treatment of politics in the play ; Mr. J. I. M. Stewart has persuasively analysed Shakespeare's presentation of Caesar ; Mr. R. A. Foakes has written on the imagery ; Mr. Ernest Schanzer has a valuable article on Brutus ; and there have been two illuminating modern editions. But there is still room for the present interesting monograph by Dr. Adrien Bonjour, of the University of Lausanne, now Professor of English at the University of Neuchâtel. He is best known, perhaps, for his work on Beowulf, and one sentence in the present book presupposes some knowledge of that poem ; but he has already published articles on several of Shakespeare's plays, and his study of *Julius Caesar* should add to his reputation as a subtle and intelligent critic. In his analysis of the structure of the play he has made a number of points which are both true and original. Occasionally, perhaps, he may seem to consider passages a little too curiously ; but his main point, on the ambivalence of Shakespeare's art, is fully convincing.

KENNETH MUIR

CONTENTS

ANTITHETICAL BALANCE AND
THE GENERAL STRUCTURE OF THE PLAY

Throughout his early historical plays, Shakespeare was powerfully attracted, if not fascinated, by the problem of political murder. His dramatic instinct prompted him to make the most of that kind of violent death and its underlying motives. Heralded (and almost out-Heroded) in *Henry VI*, political murder assumes proportions truly royal in *Richard III*. Characteristically enough it is in this first, wholly Shakespearean, ' history ' that the theme is used in its simplest terms and given its gaudiest colours. The immature young dramatist lacked restraint, and his treatment is too exaggerated to be highly effective. Richard being a consummate villain ruthlessly murders whoever—child or king—stands between him and the English crown. He therefore bears the fullest responsibility for the crimes committed, as a single individual. Even Macbeth, whose bloody record finally attains as high a level of butchery, shares the burden of crime with his wife, and is not always proof against some pricks of conscience.[1] But Richard is beyond repentance.

Shakespearean variety, however, is soon at work, and with *Richard II* political murder enters a new phase. In this drama the motive is presented with much restraint. Political murder was not actually aimed at : far from being the instrument, it was merely a by-product of a successful rebellion. The over-zealous Exton had received no orders and Bolingbroke's guilt is strictly limited. But as he is no villain he is fully aware of his own responsibility and deplores the deed. His conscience urges him " to wash this blood off from (his) guilty hand," and thus the theme of remorse is introduced, to be successfully developed in *Henry IV*.

Political crime is again prominent in the life of King John. Though the murder of Arthur, the legitimate heir, was eventually not carried out, the King clearly gave the fatal order to the killer and his moral guilt is therefore greater than Bolingbroke's. Yet it is smaller than Richard's, and in this respect John stands midway between Richard III and Henry IV. If he is more of a villain than Bolingbroke, once the disastrous consequences of

Arthur's death turn the tide against him, his repentance is sincere.

Thus, before the end of the nineties, Shakespeare had worked out, in the chronicle plays, three different types of hero involved in political murder, and his interest in the theme is only matched there by his preoccupation with the closely-connected problem of a stable government. No wonder therefore if Shakespeare, who had probably read and re-read Plutarch by the time he was writing *Henry V*, felt the lure of the most famous, earth-shaking political murder ever enacted in Roman history, and made of the story of Caesar and Brutus his first Roman tragedy. He probably saw there a magnificent opportunity for creating an entirely new type of hero involved in political crime. The three types so far developed, whether the conscience-stricken criminal *malgré lui* like Henry IV, the reticent and repentant King John, or the satanic slaughterer like Richard III, have one essential element in common. They all grew into political murderers, arrant or virtual, as a result of their pursuing selfish aims. Murder was a means either of procuring advancement or of securing the stability of an acquired position : in any case a consequence of a passion for worldly success.

Now in the greatest character among the conspirators responsible for the assassination of Caesar we meet with a man who is intrinsically noble and honest : far from wading through slaughter to a throne, his aims are disinterested. Moreover, Shakespeare deepens our interest in such an unusual character by emphasizing the purely personal aspect of the drama : that of a man who loves his benefactor and best friend, yet kills him for what he believes to be the benefit of his country : " I slew my best lover for the good of Rome!" This element—which was already in germ in Plutarch's story and therefore needed a few adjustments only—heightens the tragic character of the political crime for both the victim and the murderer as human beings. The political issue and the personal problem were thus, from the outset, ingrained in the very texture of the dramatic event, and we shall see how powerfully they were set forth by Shakespeare, with what delicate artistry he made the most of this twofold theme and made the whole tragedy hinge upon it. Besides, the story also illustrates a great theme of permanent interest which he had already learned to turn to good account : that of the turmoil which inevitably follows the violent overthrow of a ruler.

But here we may pause awhile and raise the question which needs must have preoccupied Shakespeare at some stage in his preparatory work : what were to be the limits of the tragedy? We may assume that when Shakespeare decided to include in it both the fall of Caesar and the death of Brutus, he was aware of the implications of his choice. His story is that of Caesar's murder *and* of Caesar's revenge, and including Brutus's death meant associating the tragedy of Brutus to that of Caesar so closely that one can only be thought of in terms of the other. To put it differently, Shakespeare made both tragedies more complementary even than they originally were in Plutarch, especially on the human plane. Instead of centering one play on the figure of Caesar with the conqueror's fall as a culminating point, and another around the figure of Brutus, with that hero's defeat and death as a tragic climax—so much more comfortable a pattern for some of his future critics—in other words, instead of doing dramatically what Plutarch had done narratively, his choice was for a more difficult and elegant solution : combining and condensing the drama of both great characters into one majestic sweep and thus deliberately abandoning the usual single hero structure, as he had already attempted (though with quite a different pattern) in at least one of his earlier plays. There is, in fact, no need to be so completely blinkered by the monistic (and too often dogmatic) theory of a tragic hero as not to see the consummate structure that Shakespeare achieved with his dualistic conception of this drama.[2] It is only by studying the tragedy of Caesar and the tragedy of Brutus as a close unit and showing that they cannot be dramatically dissociated, that on the contrary almost every departure from Plutarch adds to their interrelationship, that we can hope to make this clear.

For one thing, the choice is not between a confirmed tyrant and a noble, but unlucky liberator. Neither is it between a great sovereign or a ruthless conspirator or usurper : in either case there would have been no conflict in our sympathies. The choice is between two heroes, each of whom has his own greatness and his faults, each of whom in turn perplexes us, then deeply moves us, each of whom is in a way the other's victim and the other's bane. It looks indeed as if Shakespeare wanted " to prove the moral value of suspended judgment."[3] And before it is suspended, our judgment has been constantly questioned, shifted and revised : in fact, Shakespeare made of *Julius Caesar* the drama of divided sympathies.

What is, in Shakespeare, the tragedy of Caesar? If we answer bluntly that it is his death at the hands of the conspirators, it looks suspiciously like cracking a nut with a steam-hammer : indeed, the truth seems so self-evident that it does not lead us very far.[4] Unless, of course, we examine Caesar's death in all its implications and find out what Shakespeare has done with it dramatically and artistically. The harvest, then, is surprisingly rich—and the nuts to be cracked anything but hollow.

Let us first observe that a hero's violent death is, as such, not necessarily his tragedy in Shakespeare. Take Macbeth, for instance : his tragedy is not his being killed in battle, it is rather the slow, gradual, and hideous death of what was human in him. Once this is effected, and his " way of life is fall'n into the sear, the yellow leaf," what is left of Macbeth is only a soulless body, a living shell, and his fall in battle therefore leaves us cold. And Shakespeare wanted it to leave us cold : there is no dying message, as he dies off-stage (quite exceptional a death for a Shakespearean hero) and the only obituary he gets are the words " dead butcher," as brief as they are grim. With Shakespeare's Caesar, on the other hand, the situation is quite different. His death is not devoid of grandeur, nor of pathos, and it has been shrewdly observed that " in his life nothing becomes him like the leaving it ; his most dignified action is that of his death, with his face muffled in his mantle."[5] Shakespeare obviously wanted Caesar's death to be dignified, to arouse our " terror " for the deed, our pity for the man, and this explains why he actually made him innocent of the crime of tyranny. Had Caesar proved a tyrant, the whole emphasis would have been changed and the conspirators' action morally justified, even on the human plane : this is neatly illustrated in pious Richmond's address to his army before the battle of Bosworth. As Dr. Tillyard puts it, Richard III " had qualified as a tyrant ; and against an authentic tyrant it was lawful to rebel."[6] But Shakespeare's Caesar is no authentic tyrant, at worst a prospective tyrant. And since he is only a possible future tyrant, Shakespeare made of the murder an action preventive rather than punitive, and consequently Caesar a victim, not a criminal.

Brutus's famous first soliloquy, so striking a departure from (and an addition to) Plutarch, can indeed be fully explained only if we assume that Shakespeare had good grounds for not presenting Caesar as a tyrant. Though we read that the passage " has puzzled all the critics, including Coleridge and Granville-Barker "[7] it gives us one key to the tragedy of Caesar and well deserves a close attention. As to the one great critic who has not been puzzled, the disturbing shadow of modern dictators looms a little too large in his vision of Shakespeare's Caesar to allow for the actual victim behind the potential tyrant.

" It must be by his death "—the soliloquy begins with what is already Brutus's ultimate pronouncement. This opening is at the same time a conclusion and thus delicately suggests the long inner conflict which has been surging in Brutus's soul : it lends the whole monologue its real perspective and depth. The death sentence is so capital a decision that Brutus feels bound to justify it to himself, and this all the more since he has " no personal cause " against Caesar. No wonder this should have ruffled righteous republican feelings. " Had he not passed the Rubicon? Had he not entered Rome as a conqueror? Had he not placed his Gauls in the Senate?"[8] There we are precisely : Shakespeare deliberately ignores the tyrant in Caesar. Nothing could be clearer than Brutus's own admission :

> to speak truth of Caesar,
> I have not known when his affections sway'd
> More than his reason.
>
> (II. 1. 19-21)

This tribute is decisive since the failure to control his own affections (or passions) is indeed the hall-mark of the tyrant throughout Shakespeare's plays, from the early chronicles to the *Winter's Tale*. As if this were not enough yet, the point is once more harped upon at the close of the soliloquy :

> since the quarrel
> Will bear no colour for the thing he is,
> Fashion it thus. . . .
>
> (II. 1. 28-30)

There is no getting around the fact that Shakespeare made his Caesar innocent of the crime of tyranny. For no other reason, we submit, than to deepen the tragedy by showing the human victim in Caesar—before he proceeds to show it in Brutus.

Logically enough, this in turn explains the much debated problem of Shakespeare's curious emphasis on Caesar's weaknesses. We shall first focus our attention on the hero's physical ills. Here again we have both additions to, and departures from, Plutarch testifying to a deliberate design. As Dover Wilson reminds us, Shakespeare adds to the infirmities a deafness in one ear, uses the falling-sickness in a more striking context and substitutes for the hardiness praised by Plutarch a " feeble

temper."[9] So much for the facts. Now in order to avoid over-
doing the charge and unduly blackening Caesar's portrait, we
must carefully distinguish between objective reality and distorted
vision. That Caesar was deaf in his left ear is real enough since
he himself says so and, so far, we keep on solid ground. The
falling-sickness, too, is a recorded fact, and "sour" Casca
certainly enjoys disclosing the incident. But mark how different
are the reactions of Cassius and Brutus. "What, did Caesar
swound?" says Cassius, presumably in a tone reminiscent of his
spiteful sarcasm, a few minutes ago, with its emphasis on the
did's:

> I did mark
> How he did shake : 'tis true, this god did shake ;
> His coward lips did from their colour fly. . . .
> (I. i. 120-122)

Whereas on Casca's further confirmation Brutus simply remarks :
" 'Tis very like : he hath the falling-sickness." Indeed, it is quite
normal that a man should cough when he has a cold.

So it stands again with Caesar's "feeble temper". That Caesar
had a fever when he was in Spain is a matter of fact. But when
Cassius implies that Caesar was a coward because he really did
see him tremble "when the fit was on him," it gives us a mighty
measure of Cassius's blind and malignant spite—not of Caesar's
cowardice! Shakespeare so inevitably associates trembling with
either fear or fever that he uses the simile the other way round :

> Thou madest thine enemies shake, as if the world
> Were feverous and did tremble.
> (*Cor.*, I. iv. 61-62)

But we, at least, should refrain from turning the simile into an
identity : Caesar "lacks guts" only in Cassius's biased version.
The Unferthian twist in Cassius's account of the swimming
contest, moreover, should not blind us to the fact that it certainly
required much greater pluck for a man afflicted with a weak body
to plunge into the angry flood of roaring Tiber than for Cassius
himself. As Cassius is the speaker, Dover Wilson of course
acknowledges that " the points illustrate his malice", yet none
the less seems to take them at their face value when adding :
" but Brutus does not reply to the charge, and it is fully borne
out by stroke after stroke later."[10]

That Brutus does not refute the charge in no way means that

he endorses it : he only gives a provisional answer to the whole bulk of Cassius's vehement speech, and we feel that his thoughts dwell on the main point that preoccupies him, i.e., the real threat (in Caesar's popularity and power) to the liberties of Rome, rather than on minor, and obvious, distortions of his noble but " waspish " friend. No doubt he has this capital point in mind when he asks for more reflection and wants to wait until he finds a time " Both meet to hear and answer such high things." Yet, after all, we shall not be left too long in the dark as to Brutus's actual opinion and, for coming in a different context, his tribute is none the less eloquent and unmistakably proves that, on this particular point, Cassius simply could not instill into him the slightest drop of what Brutus later terms the venom of his spleen. In his address to the Roman people, the only charge he levels at Caesar is ambition, and nowhere is his honesty more patent than when he frankly recognizes what in truth belongs to Caesar. And among the dead conqueror's qualities he expressly singles out bravery : " as he was valiant, I honour him ; but as he was ambitious, I slew him. There is . . . honour for his valour ; and death for his ambition " (III. ii. 25-28). Is that a stroke confirming Cassius's charge of cowardice? Caesar's physical weaknesses, indeed, must be taken as such, without any moral blame involved.

But why, then, did Shakespeare so manifestly insist on them? What is their dramatic purpose? Dowden and the critics who followed him were certainly in the right when insisting on the contrast between Caesar's weak bodily presence and the dominant power of his spirit : " he who had been weak now rises as pure spirit, strong and terrible, and avenges himself upon the conspirators."[11] This contrast is an important element of which Brutus is aware, but which Cassius is wholly unable to grasp. That Caesar, whose bodily infirmities he despises, should have " grown so great " completely puzzles, and sorely angers him : it never occurs to him that this may have something to do with the force of Caesar's spirit.

Let us now turn to what has been called the ' thrasonical ' aspect of the hero. Dover Wilson makes much of it and insists on Caesar's moral weaknesses, i.e., " his superstition, his vacillation on the fatal morning ; and above all the profession of immovable constancy which that vacillation so ironically refutes." Concerning the last point, Kittredge thought that the purpose of Caesar's royal airs in the assassination scene " is to justify the act of the conspirators, which if our sympathies are not on their side will appear to be a cowardly assassination." Though it must be conceded that the explanation is, on the whole, pertinent enough, it should only be endorsed with some qualification. That in Casca's account and, above all, in the scene immediately preceding the murder Shakespeare, in a way, writes down Caesar is undeniable. Yet—and this is the capital point—the " writing down " is deliberately ambivalent inasmuch as it leaves room for a diametrically opposite view, and thus subtly prepares the way for the counterstroke which, sooner or later, invariably occurs and which, in writing down the conspirators, implicitly writes up Caesar's side again.[12]

But the ambivalence of Shakespeare's " writing down " of Caesar is best illustrated in the presentation of his so-called moral weaknesses. As Caesar used to speak in the third person in his own writings, it might be argued that Shakespeare simply kept that trait as historically characteristic. But since he would have refrained from doing so without good psychological or dramatic grounds, we must take the feature at its face value. First of all, within the very scenes in which the feature is most prominent,[13] two important passages occur which are certainly not meant to be disparaging, on the contrary. When Caesar answers Calpurnia's fears with the statement :

> Cowards die many times before their deaths ;
> The valiant never taste of death but once. . . .
> (II. ii. 32-33)

the phrase has a special heroic resonance the full force of which is only felt later, when illustrated in Caesar's own dignified death. This is one of the noblest touches in Shakespeare's Caesar which indirectly adds to the emotional effect produced by his corpse, when uncovered by Antony.

In the Artemidorus incident, moreover, Shakespeare, we know, went so far as to completely alter Plutarch's account of Artemidorus' failure to warn Caesar as purely accidental, to invent Caesar's striking dismissal : " What touches us ourself shall be last served."[14] This, indeed, gives us a clue to a positive aspect in Caesar's whole attitude. It points to a genuine dedication to matters political, to an almost unselfish devotion to public affairs, to a deliberate subordination of his own personal self to the ideal figure of the statesman, as he conceives it. As Mr. Stewart wrote with great penetration : " Caesar's utterances marvellously carry the impression of one physically fretted to decay, and opposing to the first falterings of the mind an increasingly rigid and absolute assertion of the Caesar-idea."[15] This marmoreal attitude, however, does not exclude a human touch, so that in the cold marble of the " immovable " Caesar there gleams a vein of richer porphyry.

This human touch comes out when Calpurnia's entreaties create a real conflict in Caesar between matters political and matters personal. When confronted with Calpurnia's passionate appeal, Caesar is persuaded that whatever danger lurks behind the ill omens, fear for his own personal safety as a man must needs submit to the necessities of the political issue at stake in the Senate. Far from being merely the testimony of a gross infatuation, of a kind of self-deification, Caesar's boasting is his only effective means of coping with what Cassius himself calls " the unaccustomed terror of this night," and its dire portents singularly amplified by Calpurnia's forebodings. " Tremble carcasse. . . ." was the famous utterance of another great captain defying human weakness in his own body on the eve of a decisive battle : Caesar defies even the mere thought of being liable to fear. He endeavours to convince his wife—and perhaps himself, too—by appealing to the ideal figure of the official and impersonal Caesar who stands, in some measure, above ordinary human condition :

> Yet Caesar shall go forth ; for these predictions
> Are to the world in general as to Caesar.
>
> (II. ii. 28-29)

Hence the constantly repeated use of the third person, pointing here to a kind of split individuality which Shakespeare most subtly underlined in that very dialogue.

Indeed, the critics who lavished their sarcasms on Caesar's " strut " here, more or less unconsciously failed to notice the moving contrast between the series of massive third person " Caesars " and the sudden return to the simple personal " I ", just when Caesar ultimately gives in to Calpurnia, who has thrown herself on her knees before him :

> Mark Antony shall say I am not well,
> And, for thy humour, I will stay at home.
>
> (II. ii. 55-56)

Try and put " Caesar " instead of " I " here and the whole point is entirely missed.[16] Thus Caesar, at this juncture, finally yields to his imploring wife—and why not also because he loves her and is moved by her? The scene is given an interesting sidelight when paralleled to Brutus's own similar conflict between his deep and disturbing political preoccupations and his affection for Portia. His deliberate and monolithic isolation suddenly thaws at the sight of Portia's self-inflicted wound. Thus there is a common streak of humanity in both great men which is most apparent when the deep love of their wives, whom they both trust, moves them to deviate for a while from the stern and straight line of political imperatives. Antony's emphasis on the human aspect of Caesar's tragedy moves us all the more because shortly before, when Caesar was at the height of his power, we caught a vivid glimpse of the humanity in him, half-hidden only behind a rigid facade. Indeed, this human streak should not be hidden from our eyes by the magnitude of the political problem.

Dover Wilson has neatly summed up the political issue : " When Brutus exclaims :

> We all stand up against the spirit of Caesar

he sums up the play in one line. For the spirit of Caesar, which was the destiny of Rome, is the fate against which Brutus struggles in vain." To Dover Wilson " the play's theme is the single one, Liberty *versus* Tyranny."[17] This may be quite right, but only on the political plane.[18] In this play, however, the political plane cannot be separated from the purely human issue—the other side of the coin. And, typically enough, the human issue is likewise hinted at in the very same sentence of Brutus :

> O, that we then could come by Caesar's spirit,
> And not dismember Caesar!
>
> > (II. i. 169-170)

Behind the clash of political ideas (and ideals) there is the bodily presence of man, who is not spirit only but also flesh and blood. The whole point means that even Brutus cannot help feeling pity for Caesar the man : though he has sided for the murder as a necessary preventive, he is more than dimly conscious that as a human being Caesar has not deserved such a bloody death. We know that for the qualified tyrant who, as such, has placed himself outside humanity, there is no great pity in Shakespeare : " Bloody thou art, bloody will be thy end." And when the end has come, and Richard's knell has tolled : " the bloody dog is dead." How different here : " alas, Caesar must bleed for it."

The theme is given singular force when taken over unawares,

at a decisive moment, in the very last sentences of a Caesar already
surrounded by the conspirators : the world, he says, is

> furnish'd well with men,
> And men are flesh and blood, and apprehensive.
> (III. i. 66-7)

This is fine dramatic irony : within a minute, indeed, his own
poor, weak body is going to bleed to death, hacked to pieces by
a whole group of incensed murderers. And simple human pity
for Caesar's bleeding body—a sentiment which is to play so capital
a part in the next scenes—is all the more easily aroused and
heightened in that we have been made aware (and how vividly)
that, however " prodigious grown," the mighty conqueror is also
only a man, like any other Roman, bound to a body which is
flesh and blood. More than anything else his weak body now
makes us fully realize his human condition. The conqueror at
the height of his glory, who did bestride the world like a colossus
and has become the State incorporate, is also but a man—and
" this for him is tragedy enough,"[19] since men are flesh and blood,
and therefore submitted, whether conqueror or commoner, to
all the evils that flesh is heir to : partial deafness, fits of fever,
falling-sickness and now, finally, mortal wounds " spouting forth
blood." All his glories are now shrunk to this little measure—
" no worthier than the dust," cries Brutus, " a bleeding piece of
earth," chimes in Antony. On this point friend and assassin are
at one!

Such a pitiful end, moreover, for a crime he had not even
committed. And this it is which ultimately condemns Brutus.
His bloody deed might have been justified against a real tyrant.
But here, though Caesar *might* have turned a tyrant and the
preventive deed might have proved politically advisable, on the
personal plane it definitely transgresses the human law. Hence
Antony's malediction :

> Woe to the hand that shed this costly blood!
> (III. i. 259)

Hence the apparition of Caesar's ghost which unmistakably points
to a wronged soul. From now on, pity for Caesar's body grows
deeper and deeper. Before it is used as an effective ferment to
rouse the Roman people, it is profoundly felt, and movingly
expressed, in Antony's great monologue. In the present play,
at least, all sentiments expressed in a soliloquy are genuine, and

Antony's words, when left alone before the bleeding body of his friend, are the full expression of a deep sorrow. That sentiment had to be shown at its purest, on the human plane, before it was turned to good account on the political plane. Otherwise Antony might have appeared as a pure (and most clever) politician only, whereas he also is a man hurt in his affections, weeping for a friend he cherished.

Shakespeare meant Antony's love to be taken seriously. He makes it a fact recognized even by his enemy Cassius who mentions " the ingrafted love he bears to Caesar." Antony, indeed, is the most human of the great characters in *Julius Caesar*, and it is just a gentle Shakespearean touch to have made him both a nimble-footed and quick-spirited man, a reveller who loves plays and music. His famous speech, the purple patch of the play, is all the more effective because we know that Antony's grief and pity are not shammed : after they have been given a most natural and spontaneous outlet in the monologue, these sentiments are now canalized and made into a powerful instrument of revenge against the murderers, so great is their impact upon the Roman people. It is because the bloody deed transgressed the human law and made of Caesar the man a victim that his wounds—" poor poor dumb mouths "—become so eloquent.[20] The spectacular reversal which means that the tide has now turned against Brutus and the conspirators (just when they thought they had taken it " at the flood ") thus partakes of the personal, quite as much as of the political, plane.

That this is true for the whole anticlimax can best be brought home by conjuring up the spirit of Caesar. In the most stimulating part of his introduction to the play, Dover Wilson emphatically equates it with Caesarism. Now the spirit of Caesar has a twofold aspect, and we have reasons to believe that Shakespeare deliberately intended the ambivalence. There is no doubt that in Brutus's outcry " We all stand up against the spirit of Caesar," we have a reference to Caesarism, or at least to an ambition that might endanger the liberty of the Roman people. This, of course, crystallizes the political theme of the play. Brutus's dilemma resides in the impossibility to dissociate that spirit from the man himself : he cannot do away with the threat of autocracy without doing away with Caesar the man—and as a man he both loves and respects him. But once he has decided the issue and sacrifices the human being in Caesar to what he thinks a higher political imperative, it is precisely that subordinated human quantum which bears the seed of his own defeat—and it spells defeat by shattering first Brutus's precarious edifice and, ultimately, the man Brutus himself. For the personal wrong he did to Caesar, much more than Caesarism, determines the great reflux, seals the fate of the conspirators and leads Brutus to his fall.[21]

The shift is obvious if we examine the second reference to the spirit of Caesar. It occurs immediately after Antony has solemnly shaken hands with each of the conspirators. Suddenly turning to Caesar's body, in their own presence, Antony cries out :

> That I did love thee, Caesar, O, 'tis true :
> If then thy spirit look upon us now,
> Shall it not grieve thee dearer than thy death,
> To see thy Antony making his peace,
> Shaking the bloody fingers of thy foes,
> Most noble! in the presence of thy corse?
> Had I as many eyes as thou hast wounds,
> Weeping as fast as they stream forth thy blood,
> It would become me better than to close
> In terms of friendship with thine enemies.
> Pardon me, Julius!
>
> (III. i. 195-205)

We have quoted the passage because it clearly shows that the emphasis is now on the personal, not the political, element. The spirit of Caesar who looks upon the scene no longer stands for Caesarism : it is the individual spirit of the man Caesar, rising over his bleeding body, the spirit of a human victim—not a political entity.

This could not have been more subtly conveyed than by the skilful transition, on Antony's lips, from *Caesar* at the beginning of the address to *Julius* at the close. And mark how the individual element is stressed in the very contrast between the words *you, your, yours*, which occur seven times in the first seven lines to the conspirators, and the words *thou, thee, thy*, repeated no less than seventeen times in the seventeen lines to Caesar's body . . . and spirit! This accumulation almost works like an incantation, and the carefully balanced opposition between " thy spirit " and " thy corse", " thy Antony " and " thy foes " within the same sentence anticipates the very issue behind the great reflux. The theme of revenge, indeed, is announced immediately afterwards, as soon as Antony is left alone and again begs Caesar's pardon for being " gentle with these butchers." But this time Antony's grief and pity at the sight of Caesar's body are topped by a great prophecy : the costly blood shed by the conspirators will ask for more blood, the spectre of civil strife will rise over a torn and bleeding Italy,

> And Caesar's spirit ranging for revenge,
> With Ate by his side come hot from hell,
> Shall in these confines with a monarch's voice
> Cry ' Havoc,' and let slip the dogs of war.
>
> (III. i. 271-4)

How this prophecy inexorably proves true is the argument of the second part of the drama. When Antony tells us that he will try, in his oration,

> how the people take
> The cruel issue of these bloody men,
>
> (III. i. 294-5)

we understand that he is to be himself the instrument of Caesar's vengeance, to whose spirit he might have said :

> I do but stay behind
> To do the office for thee of revenge.

With this third reference to Caesar's spirit we are back again in the world of political events. We know that, however personal its motivation, Caesar's revenge will be enacted on the great political stage, and at this juncture both planes coalesce. The perfect balance between the personal and the political planes is, in fact, one of the finest achievements of this tragedy. No doubt the political issue looms large enough, whether on the Capitol, in the quarrel scene, or on the battlefield of Philippi. That it is, however, but one side of the medal is shown by three departures from Plutarch which are of no mean interest.

The first, and more obvious, is Shakespeare's transformation of the spirit visiting Brutus into Caesar's ghost. Even if such an identification was already traditional and therefore not actually Shakespeare's invention, the dramatist uses it with a definite purpose. We know that the brief appearance of Caesar's spirit has suffered from a comparison with the much more elaborated apparitions of the elder Hamlet. Even if we do not assign Hamlet's father as capital a part in the drama as Dr. Flatter has done, there is no doubt that, compared with the majestic ghost of buried Denmark, Caesar's spirit indeed seems somewhat insignificant. There cannot be any uncertainty, however, as to the meaning of the ghost: it is the perturbed spirit of a man who has been grievously wronged and cannot rest until that wrong is fully avenged.

What makes this clear—more than any parallel with Hamlet's father or with Banquo—is Brutus's own decisive testimony. Characteristically enough, this twofold testimony represents a Shakespearean addition to Plutarch which cannot be considered as a traditional trait. When Brutus and his poor remains of friends are definitely driven to bay in the *débâcle* of Philippi, these are his words to induce Volumnius to kill him, lest he should fall into his enemies' hands:

> The ghost of Caesar hath appear'd to me
> Two several times by night; at Sardis once,
> And this last night here in Philippi fields:
> I know my hour is come.
> (V. v. 17-20)

More even than a disastrous defeat on a battlefield, the apparition of Caesar's ghost is now to Brutus the real sign of his imminent end: his life, like Cassius's, " is run his compass." Could the idea of Nemesis have been more vividly conveyed, and does this not again imply Caesar's innocence?[22] If Shakespeare's Caesar were in fact a tyrant or, worse still, the universal dictator, and had " disjoined remorse from power," as Dover Wilson suggests,[23] there would have been no sense in such an apparition—or a sense so different that it would make bitter irony of Brutus's dying words. Whereas those moving words,

> Caesar, now be still:
> I kill'd not thee with half so good a will,
> (V. v. 50-1)

rather show Brutus's consciousness of the wrong he has committed towards Caesar the man. Behind the readiness to kill himself lurks the feeling that the act meets the demands of some kind of immanent justice: now only can Caesar's spirit " be still "—and with this act only has Caesar's tragedy come to a close. The balance is restored. The great moral lesson of the play can be expressed in two Shakespearean lines:

> There is no sure foundation set on blood,
> No certain life achieved by others' death.[24]

But Brutus has now expiated for Caesar's precious blood. He

has, in a way, redeemed himself—and heroically at that. Hence the tragedy can close on Antony's fine tribute :

> His life was gentle, and the elements
> So mix'd in him that Nature might stand up
> And say to all the world ' This was a man !
>
> (V. v. 73-5)

That Shakespeare has put this beautiful tribute (the third of the additions to Plutarch we have just mentioned) precisely in Antony's mouth, is of the highest significance.

Antony, we know, expressed a genuine grief at Caesar's death and a real horror at the bloody deed from a purely human point of view.[25] His prophecy (now completely fulfilled) gave us a foreboding that Brutus's conscious sacrifice of the human element to the political issue would eventually turn against Brutus's own cause and against Brutus, the man, himself. Antony thus personified the human revolt against a crime which might have been politically justifiable but could not be humanly justified. But since Brutus has now paid the penalty not only on the political plane (his precipitate flight into exile) but also on the human level (his suicide), the conflict is resolved, the score is evened, Caesar's perturbed spirit may rest in peace—and nothing prevents Antony " with his instinctive grasp of human values " from rendering unto Brutus the man what belongeth to Brutus.

At the same time, of course, Antony's final tribute is a last vivid flash into the very heart of Brutus's own tragedy. And to this tragedy, which finds it conclusion simultaneously with that of Caesar, we must now turn. Both are so closely interwoven that they are not dramatically separable in Shakespeare, though they could be narratively separated in Plutarch ; and thus, by dealing with the one, we have implicitly dealt with the other to a very large extent. Suffice it, therefore, to stress a few important points which have, so far, remained in the background of our discussion.

We briefly mentioned Brutus's dilemma. We have a right to assume that he was perfectly conscious of the difficulties and drawbacks of a choice, that he weighed the pros and cons and only reached his final decision after a long inner debate. In fact, Marvin Felheim's analysis of time in the present play makes it clear that a whole month elapsed between the moment when Cassius first whetted Brutus against Caesar and the death verdict in the monologue.[26] That this month was " a particularly trying one for Brutus," we may well believe since the conflict within him deprived him of his sleep ; and that his final decision, moreover, implied a sacrifice, and was to his mind only the lesser evil, is confirmed by his attempt at justifying the deed towards his own conscience, before proceeding to justify it towards public opinion. Now this private settlement of Brutus's moral conflict, which provides him with the necessary basis for future action, is of the utmost importance and clearly brings out the fundamental flaw in his position. " So far, Brutus admits, Caesar had not shown himself the tyrant : but then he has not yet attained ' the upmost round ' of the ladder. Once thus high he will scorn ' the base degrees by which he did ascend '. Once crowned, all barriers will be down : and, human nature being what it is, ' the bright day will bring forth the adder ', since absolute rulers have no use for mercy (' remorse ')."[27]

Dover Wilson, who gives us this excellent summing up of the case, is right in refusing to see there anything perplexing, confused or fumbling. Yet we should be careful not to judge of the issue from the political angle only. Psychologically, Brutus's diagnosis is sound enough : " So Caesar may," indeed. But when he adds " Then lest he may, prevent," he takes a decisive step which raises the whole moral question of the legitimacy of the murder not only on the political, but also on the human plane—and here we may well wonder whether man can be morally killed on the strength of a *may*![28] Brutus says ' yes ' because he feels he must sacrifice Caesar, his friend, for what he thinks the good of Rome. But Brutus feels that it will not do to kill him like a criminal— " Or else were this a savage spectacle!" In other words he feels the necessity of a way out because he more or less consciously realizes that, however sound it seems to him politically, this " dreadful thing " transgresses the human law. What is his solution?

Now, though we must needs avoid hacking our way through the " veritable thickets of contemporary opinion " which rightly alarm a recent reviewer,[29] we feel bound to give at least some critical Caesars their due—and, on this point, no one has shed more light than Professor Brents Stirling in one of his latest articles. Brutus's way out, he shows, is " to dignify assassination . . . by lifting it to a level of rite and ceremony."[30] That is why (to add a further touch to Brents Stirling's convincing demonstration) Brutus insists on paying a public homage to Caesar's qualities : being fair to Caesar's " better parts " will deprive the act of any personal connotation and make the conspirators' purpose " necessary and not envious." As will be immediately noticed,

there is the same basic fallacy in Brutus's public justification of
the deed as in the private settlement of his inner conflict.

When Brutus says :

> since the quarrel
> Will bear no colour for the thing he is,
> Fashion it thus ; that what he is, augmented,
> Would run to these and these extremities
> (II. i. 28-31).

he frankly recognizes that since reality (what Caesar *is*) is not
sufficient to warrant the death verdict, it must be so " fashioned "
as to make the deed appear really justifiable. But then, by
definitely basing the whole action on what *would be*, instead of on
what *is*, he unwittingly clothes reality with appearance. Now
Brutus's need for ceremony to " purify the violent act of all taint
of butchery and raise it to the level of sacrifice " clearly shows
his concern for public opinion ; in his statement about the
sacrificial method of killing Caesar, " Brutus has allowed his
great invocation to shift into a concluding note on policy . . . we
shall thus 'appear' to the citizenry as purgers, not murderers."
But thereby, further to quote Brents Stirling, " he ' unconsciously '
reveals the very evasion which Antony later amplifies ruthlessly :
to transmute political killing into ritual is to cloak it with appear-
ances."[31] This is perfectly clear. But why is Brutus so intent on
making the deed *appear* justifiable (both towards his own
conscience and public opinion) if not precisely because that piece
of political killing was not actually justified on the purely human
level, too, Caesar being still innocent of the crime of tyranny?

The strength of Antony's position is that he can see through
the facade of ritual and ceremony and demolish it by a devastating
stroke by simply appealing to what, for him, is reality enough :
Caesar's innocence. To him Caesar *is* a human victim, and his
murderers *are* therefore butchers. And thus, in his great speech
(which, however subtle and consummate its oratory, expresses
his own genuine sentiments) Caesar's poor clay, " no worthier
than the dust," is turned into powerful and passionate clay,
accusing his assassins and moving the very " stones of Rome to
rise and mutiny." The great political reversal is accomplished,
Brutus's public position is shattered. But if he has paid on the
political level, Brutus has not yet made up for Caesar's blood on
the human level—and destiny decrees that this debt can only be
paid by his own death, as he finally realizes after the double

apparition of Caesar's ghost. Crime and punishment have thus been inexorably connected, and with Brutus's suicide the wheel has come full circle.

The tragic element, however, somewhat transcends what we might call that fateful balance of the " audit ": Shakespeare makes us feel that though Brutus is, in a way, responsible for his own end, he is none the less, like Caesar, a victim. Indeed, few outcries are more pathetic than his dying words :

> Caesar, now be still :
> I kill'd not thee with half so good a will.
> (V. v. 50-1)

It would probably lead us too far to do full justice to Brutus as a victim, so subtle is Shakespeare's characterization, so delicate the balance between sympathy and irony. We must be content to single out one trait which proves how inextricable the situation was for him once he had finally decided how to solve the terrible dilemma.

As we have seen, it is quite obvious that Brutus does not act for self-advancement, or more generally for personal aims. This, of course, puts him into a class apart, not only as against the rest of the conspirators, but even as against all the political murderers who precede him in Shakespeare's plays. This is evidently the main factor which deepens the tragedy of Brutus's death. That his disaster has its essential cause in the deliberate sacrifice of the human to the political element, we have tried to make clear. But once the sacrifice decided upon, Brutus does his best to limit the violent action to the barest minimum :

> Publius, good cheer ;
> There is no harm intended to your person,
> Nor to no Roman else : so tell them, Publius.
> (III. i. 90-2)

He insists on sparing Mark Antony, thereby waving aside the most elementary precaution which the action against Caesar required. The dramatic irony is, of course, that this gentle restraint of his, this disregard of the realistic imperatives conditioning the act of violence, simply pave the way for his own defeat, together with that of the republican cause.

Before we examine the implications of the point, we must briefly dwell on Brutus's concern for public opinion. Brents Stirling calls attention to it in an interesting note, and there is

no denying that Brutus is far from being " as austerely un-
concerned about public favor " as is commonly assumed. He
declares that killing Antony would make the course " seem too
bloody," insists that the action against Caesar ought to appear
necessary " to the common eyes," and is persuaded that the
conditions upon which Antony is to speak at the funeral " shall
advantage more than do us wrong." As to Brutus's address to
the Roman people, we quite agree with Brents Stirling that " a
re-reading of it will scarcely disclose aloofness or an avoidance
of popular emotive themes."[32] On the contrary, at the close of
his speech Brutus actually goes as far as to resort to what might
be called the dagger trick : " as I slew my best lover for the good
of Rome, I have the same dagger for myself, when it shall please
my country to need my death." This is, after all, no very far
cry from Caesar's own theatrical gesture—to the same Roman
crowd—which roused sour Casca's sardonic humour.[33] This
unmistakably shows a touch of the realist in Brutus which might
well appear a little surprizing at first sight.

There is no doubt that this concern about public favour is
genuine and no mere persuasive argument presented to his
fellow-conspirators, who are more likely to be convinced by
such opportunistic grounds than by purely moral considerations.
However unshakable his integrity, once he has decided on a
political action of great magnitude, Brutus, who is no fool, feels
bound to make allowance for public opinion. But this is not the
main point. What matters is whether this genuine concern also
corresponds to his own inner feelings, or whether it testifies to
a touch of what the Bastard Faulconbridge would call Commodity. In other words, is there a discrepancy between Brutus's
public attitude and his private opinion? Obviously not : as a
matter of fact Brutus is the only character in the great quartet
who tunes his actions throughout in harmony with his personal
convictions. The titular hero (as has been pertinently expressed)
builds " above his weaknesses the conception of the impersonal
Caesar, unshaken, unseduced, unterrified."[34] Cassius deliberately
deceives his own friend Brutus and uses a cheap stratagem to win
him over ; and in one scene, at least, Antony proves a pure
adept in Commodity in his treatment of Lepidus.[35] But Brutus
never bows to Commodity, and when he wishes to spare Antony
because the conspirators' cause would seem too bloody, we are
aware that this is no actual concession to public opinion, that
this corresponds to his own inward sentiment and that he is

thus perfectly sincere in his wish to avoid what he thinks super-
fluous bloodshed. To him it was already tragical enough to have
Caesar " bleed for it." Likewise, when he resorts to the dagger
trick, we also know that he is not playing a part, at bottom, but
is quite ready to kill himself for the good of Rome.

As must be repeated, it is not the least aspect of his tragedy
that he should fail precisely because he is the only one whose
public attitude and actions conform to his own private moral
code. " Since he judges the wisdom of a course of action not
by its probable results in the world of events, but by its effect
upon his peace of mind, his decisions are grave practical mistakes."
His career could therefore be described as " a history of the
mistakes in which his rigid application of stoical principles
involve him."[36] As we have said before, his situation is inextricable because he is too honest to accept the full implications of
the terrible action on the level of political events. Though he
has been driven to choose a solution which meant an essentially
indiscriminate deed—the violent and bloody overthrow of a
ruler—the stamp of his character urges him to apply discriminate
means (such as sparing Antony) when coping with an ensuing
external situation which called for ruthless, drastic measures.

Shakespeare actually manages to put this point into relief by
providing a subtle foil to Brutus's position in Antony's own
attitude, when confronted with a somewhat similar problem. So
skilful and unobtrusive is Shakespeare's artistry here that we
only realize this half-consciously.

Deeply hurt in his sentiments and revolted at the bloody action
which cruelly struck at what to him was an innocent man, Antony
dedicates himself to the stern mission of avenging Caesar. And
here, typically enough, he loses no time in establishing the degree
of Brutus's responsibility as against that of the rest of the conspirators (though he certainly knows that Brutus acted on different
motives). Antony's very first sentence in his soliloquy immediately shows that he makes no discrimination between the
murderers but puts them all in the same boat.

> O, pardon me, thou bleeding piece of earth,
> That I am meek and gentle with *these butchers*![37]
>
> (III. i. 225-6)

In just the same way he later refers to " The cruel issue of *these
bloody men*." In his famous speech, the full weight of his attack
is more specifically directed against Brutus, because he feels that

Brutus's position, which is prominent enough, is all the stronger owing to his personal integrity. And thus the whole trend of his attack tends to reduce Brutus to exactly the same level as the other conspirators, i.e., a mere butcher, with the aggravating clause of sheer ingratitude.

Nowhere is this more characteristic than in his wily insinuation as to the personal reasons which may have led the murderers to do away with Caesar :

> They that have done this deed are honourable ;
> What *private griefs* they have, alas, I know not
> That made them do it.
>
> (III. ii. 212-14)

Whereas we know (and he knows) that Brutus, at least, had no " private grief " against Caesar. But remembering how Brutus precisely sought to depersonalize the deed, we may regard it as magnificent *realpolitik* on Antony's part to affect seeking the grounds of the political crime in the conspirators' personal motives. He instinctively understands that his cause—the mission of revenge to which he has dedicated himself—asks for no discrimination between the murderers as long as it has not been accomplished. That is why, just before the decisive battle, Antony attacks the murderers for the last time and, again, makes no distinction between Brutus and the rest of them :

> Villains, you did not so, when your vile daggers
> Hack'd one another in the sides of Caesar :
> You show'd your teeth like apes, and fawned like hounds,
> And bow'd like bondmen, kissing Caesar's feet ;
> Whilst damned Casca, like a cur, behind
> Struck Caesar on the neck. O you flatterers ![38]
>
> (V. i. 39-44)

It is only when the mission is successfully carried out, and Caesar's murder completely avenged, that Antony can afford to discriminate and put Brutus into a special category (apart from *all* the other conspirators) by paying him a supreme homage :

> This was the noblest Roman of them all :
> All the conspirators, *save only he*,
> Did that they did in envy of great Caesar ;
> *He only*, in a general honest thought
> And common good to all, made one of them.
>
> (V. v. 68-72)

A homage all the more significant in that it comes from a man who had to fight against him till he was destroyed.[39] The contrast with Brutus's own attitude towards Antony could not have been more subtly intimated.

Yet, if Brutus's sparing of Antony actually proved a grave practical mistake, the main instrument of his ultimate defeat, Brutus is morally the greater for it, and we feel that Antony's tribute is perfectly deserved.

Pregnant as it is, and brilliantly justified from a psychological viewpoint, Antony's tribute has at the same time a structural purpose : it is, in fact, the counterpart of Brutus's own praise of Caesar. The striking parallelism is that in both cases the greatness of the fallen hero is recognized by the very man who was most instrumental in his fall. And, as befits those tragic characters who, whatever their failings, are the greater for their death, and die as noble human victims, both are honoured with the supreme touch of dignified obsequies.[40] Just as Brutus himself begged his countrymen to " Do grace to Caesar's corpse," now Caesar's heir, Octavius, orders Brutus's remains to be used according to his virtue " with all respect and rites of burial."

Finally, Antony's tribute is the last swing of the pendulum, bringing to a standstill the constantly alternating movement of our sympathies from one hero, or party, to the other.[41] After he had written Brutus down in the Forum scene, Shakespeare " then wrote Brutus and Cassius up again more and more from that moment until the catastrophe."[42] With one exception, however. Just before the decisive battle, which is to show us in a series of impressionistic and impressive touches Brutus and his followers at bay . . . and at their best, we are reminded of the worse aspect of Caesar's murder. More vividly even than when it was enacted, we sharply realize with Antony's biting attack by what unfair, treacherous means Caesar was trapped and stabbed. Shakespeare knew that since our sympathies irresistibly turn to the vanquished in the stirring scenes of Philippi, there might have been a serious threat of their being simultaneously withdrawn from the opposite side. He therefore deftly managed to forestall this on the one hand by means of this short retrospect of Caesar's murder, on the other hand by stressing the real justice of the victors' cause at the very apex of their triumph. That last reminder of Brutus's transgression of the human law was thus particularly apposite. But now, as Brutus has fully expiated his deed, the tragedy may close on what is the highest praise ever bestowed on him in the whole course of the play. And Antony's eulogy, together with his preceding, and last, attack, represent the final great point-counterpoint of the tragedy.

Yet, fittingly enough, Antony's tribute is ambivalent, too, inasmuch as it testifies to his own essential nobility and magnanimity, and therefore indirectly, but supremely, writes him up. This time, however, the ambivalence is entirely positive, since both parties are thus exalted at the same time, and the opposition between the conflicting sides is now resolved. Needless to say, this dignified and moving touch calls forth, in spite of the tragic end, a kind of elation mainly due to our sentiment that the hero's death has retrieved his faults, has made him nobler, and greater.

* * *

Reduced to its simplest terms, *Julius Caesar* is the story of a political murder and a posthumous revenge. A dramatic story where the victim of the murder turns into the soul of the revenge, and the murderer himself into the avenger's victim. A drama where a great political issue and a purely personal problem are mingled like flesh and blood—and the flesh cannot be cut through without shedding the costly blood. The tragedy is that, however noble its underlying motives, a bloody deed does bring " a curse upon the minds of men ": a violent overthrow brings on more violence —blood, destruction and civil strife overwhelm in a mighty wave the whole body of the state, and the wave only subsides when the wheel has come full circle and the curse lights upon the doer of the deed. But the tragedy is also that we are emotionally attracted, and repulsed, by both sides : our sympathies are made to oscillate from one hero, and one party, to the other, according to the side of the Roman medal we are shown, obverse and then reverse, until the swing of the pendulum eventually ceases, suspended as it were between two equal forces, and then the sympathies are perfectly divided between the victim of the crime and the victim of the punishment. In both cases Man is the loser—and that's the pity of it all—but there is some solace yet for the heroical loser in that he wins some posthumous glory.

In short it is a drama with opposing elements so mixed in it that its antithetical theme and its antithetical motives form its very texture. The balance is highly structural, and the inner structure is so highly balanced that it reaches in its very ambivalence a grand simplicity. And such simplicity has—to transpose a Huxleyan phrase—the rigor, and the beauty, of a syllogism carved in porphyry.

Notes on Chapter 1

[1] Indeed, according to Professor Muir's happy formula, " Richard is the villain as hero ; Macbeth is a hero who becomes a villain." *Macbeth*, ed. K. Muir (London, 1951), p. lxi.

[2] If we can dispense with making a complete survey of critical opinion (and divergences) as to the structure of *Julius Caesar*, a few considerations on this point may not be unnecessary here. As can be expected, the play has suffered from the monistic preconception, and most critics have tried to save the principle of a single tragic hero by forcing either Caesar or Brutus into the dominant figure of the drama. In doing so they have unduly emphasized the dramatic role of either character at the expense of the other, and the whole controversy results in the somewhat paradoxical situation that the supporters of Brutus have been more successful in arguing against Caesar as the real hero, than they have been in arguing for their own conception, and vice versa.

A few critics have deliberately abandoned the single hero structure in favour of a study in character grouping, based on four leading figures. Set forth by Moulton (*Shakespeare as a Dramatic Artist*, 3. ed., Oxford, 1906, p. 169) this conception seems to have been partly revived by Sir Mark Hunter : " The personal interest in this play, the appeal of individual character, is not concentrated, as it is in the normally constructed tragedies, on one dominant figure which over-shadows all the rest. It is distributed . . . for on the stage no one of these characters dominates the action throughout. The first act of the tragedy is Cassius' act ; the second is Brutus'; the third is Antony's ; and in the fourth and fifth Cassius and Brutus together make a joint tragic appeal " (" Politics and Character in Shakespeare's ' Julius Caesar ' ", *Essays by Divers Hands*, X, London, 1931, 114-115). If the rejection of one single dominant figure is structurally sound, we suggest that such a distribution of characters among the five acts of the play is not the right alternative, and does not fit the architecture of the drama. Moreover, it no longer makes sense to speak of a Shakespearean play as a normally, or abnormally, constructed tragedy. As cannot be too strongly emphasized, " Every play that he wrote is unique in that it has its own particular problem of construction and its own solution " (H. T. Price, " Construction in Shakespeare ", *University of Michigan Contributions in Modern Philology*, No. 17, 1951, 1. This was already stressed by Moody E. Prior, who insists that " Each play must be regarded as a unique problem." Cf. *The Language of Tragedy*, New York, 1947, pp. 73-74). The critic, however, who seems to come closer to the views submitted in the present essay is Lorenz Morsbach, who considers the play as " die Darstellung einer grossen geschichtlichen Begebenheit, ein Ereignisdrama, in welchem Cäsar und Brutus eine gleich hervorragende Rolle spielen, Cäsar im ersten, Brutus im zweiten

Teile. Das Drama hat zwei Höhepunkte, die geschichtlich als Ursache u. Folge zusammenhängen und vom Dichter auch zu einer künstlerischen Einheit verknüpft sind" ("Shakespeares Cäsarbild", *Studien zur Englischen Philologie*, LXXXVIII, Halle, 1935, 5). Of very recent work on *Julius Caesar*, Mr. T. S. Dorsch's edition in the Revised Arden Shakespeare (1955) appeared after my manuscript had been sent to the printer, and could therefore not be used. Mr. E. Schanzer's interesting article ("The Tragedy of Shakespeare's Brutus", *ELH*, XXII (1955), 1-15), also appeared too late to be used. It is clear, however, that we independently agree on a number of points, and differ only on the question of the hero.

3 D. A. Stauffer, *Shakespeare's World of Images* (New York, 1949), p. 111.

4 See, however, J. V. Cunningham, "'Tragedy' in Shakespeare", *ELH*, XVII (1950), 36-46.

5 *Julius Caesar*, ed. H. H. Furness Jr., New Variorum Shakespeare (Philadelphia, 1913), p. viii.

6 E. M. W. Tillyard, *Shakespeare's History Plays*, 3. imp. (London, 1951), p. 212. King James I himself ultimately seems to admit it, too. Though cautiously declaring that rebellion, even against a tyrant king, is "ever unlawfull" on the subjects' part, he acknowledges that "his fall is little meaned by the rest of his Subiects, and . . . it oft falleth out, that the commiters not onely escape unpunished, but farther, *the fact will remaine as allowed by the Law in divers aages thereafter*" (Quoted by Muir, *ed. cit.*, p. lxii, from the *Basilikon Doron*. Italics mine). Cf. L. B. Campbell, "Political Ideas in *Macbeth*, IV, iii,"*SQ*, II (1951), 281-286.

7 *Julius Caesar*, ed. J. Dover Wilson, New Shakespeare (Cambridge, 1949), p. xxx.

8 Coleridge's famous perplexed outcry, quoted by Furness, *Caesar*, p. 73.

9 Dover Wilson, *Caesar*, p. xxviii.

10 *Ibid.* Dover Wilson is probably right when interpreting "feeble temper" as referring to Caesar's "temperament" rather than to his "bodily weakness", as glossed by Kittredge. Yet Shakespeare himself only stresses the physical aspect of Caesar's infirmities and Cassius it is who passionately equates them with a feeble temper, thus completely blurring the distinction—nay the obvious contrast—between Caesar's weak body and powerful spirit. This is a brilliant touch characterizing Cassius, when grief and blood ill-tempered vexeth him, and passion blindfolds him to an evidence of which his much more objective and clear-headed friend Brutus is fully aware.

11 E. Dowden, *Shakspere : His Mind and Art*, 13. ed. (London, 1906), p. 287. Yet Dowden only brings out "the contrast between the weakness of Caesar's bodily presence in the first half of the play, and the might of his spiritual presence in the latter half of the play" (*ibid.*),

whereas even in the former part we may detect a few, but unmistakable, traits hinting at Casesar's spiritual strength, opposed to his physical weakness.

[12] That is why, incidentally, so good a case can be made in favour of, as well as against, Caesar—or Brutus, for that matter. " Casca's travesty of the ceremonial offering of the crown and of the token offering by Caesar of his throat for cutting " (Brents Stirling, *PMLA*, LXVI (1951), 768), effective as it is, loses some of its impact since we are aware that it comes from a man reputed as " sour " among his very friends, and who bears a grudge against Caesar. Furthermore, what arouses Casca's spite more than anything else is that both ceremonial offerings are highly successful with the Roman crowd, so that a good part of his sarcasms is also levelled at the simple Roman citizens. (Mark especially the contemptuous terms he uses with reference to the commoners: " the rabblement ", " the tag-rag people ", " the common herd ", as well as the ironical " their worships " contrasted with the immediately following " three or four wenches "). Now there is irony in the fact that this very same crowd responds with stormy applause to Brutus's own ceremonial, conferring the dignity of a sacrificial rite on the murder of Caesar. This retrospectively throws into relief the highly relative value of Casca's attack. Moreover, a counterpart of Casca's travesty—this time in favour of the opposite party—is to be found in Antony's ironical words, subtly hinting at the sacrificial murder ; so that here again (slightly to transpose Brents Stirling's phrase) serious ritual has been brought into great prominence and then subjected to scornful commentary, or hints. (Brents Stirling, *op. cit.*, 770, points out that Antony's " mockery in counter-ritual " consists in " a threefold repetition, ' kneel ', ' fall down ', and ' being prostrate ', which brings the ceremonial irony close to a level of satire.")

[13] And it seems so above all in his dialogue with his wife, where it strikes us as being more histrionic than anywhere else since it is Casesar the husband, and not the public figure, who speaks.

[14] See M. W. MacCallum, *Shakespeare's Roman Plays and their Background* (London, 1910), p. 226.

[15] J. I. M. Stewart, *Character and Motive in Shakespeare* (London, 1949), p. 53. As Mr. Stewart further observes, Shakespeare " is leading the judicious to discern that the overwhelming, immediate and public Caesar is the creation of an inflexible will, is a rigid mask which has proved so potent that its creator himself can scarcely regard it but with awe."

[16] After this significant opposition Caesar, as a rule, keeps to the personal " I ". In the ensuing conversation with Decius and Calpurnia he uses it eleven times (II, ii, 62-107) and only lapses twice into the third person. And in one of these two instances at least we have again a reminder of the ideal and impersonal Caesar : " Shall Caesar send a lie?"

[17] Dover Wilson, *Caesar*, pp. xxi-xxii.

[18] But even on the purely political plane a strong case can be made against that somewhat simplified conception. Thus *Julius Caesar*, together with *Antony and Cleopatra*, has been said to illustrate a "fundamental principle of Renaissance thinking about the nature and structure of states." Politically this principle stating that "the speciality of rule must be exercised by a single authority, not divided among several," is opposed to the conspirators' "concept of aristocratic sovereignty," and consequently the assassination of Caesar is no less than " the violation of normal political order " (J. E. Phillips, *The State in Shakespeare's Greek and Roman Plays*, New York, 1940, pp. 172, 204). To this should be added Maria Wickert's interesting conception of the tragedy : " Das Cäsardrama beruht auf einer Verbindung der Tragödie des Übermenschen mit der Gattung der Rachetragödie. Die Provokation die in Cäsars Übermenschentum liegt, ist der eigentliche Anlass zu seiner Ermordung, nicht eine politische Ideologie " (" Antikes Gedankengut in Shakespeares Julius Cäsar," *Sh. Jahr.*, Bd. 82/83, 1948, 31). See also A. F. Fairchild, *Shakespeare and the Tragic Theme* (Columbia, 1944), p. 21.

[19] We here take the liberty of transferring to Caesar the phrase which Professor Tolkien first applied to Beowulf—in quite different circumstances—in his famous British Academy lecture on the poem.

[20] And here, of course, this eloquence is heightened by the reminder of Casesar's love to Brutus which made of the latter's stroke " the most unkindest cut of all." The horror and the inhumanity of that one stab could hardly be more vividly conveyed than by the blood motive, a mute testimony of the revolt of man—nay of man's very flesh and blood—against such criminal ingratitude. It looks, indeed, as if Caesar had been doubly killed.

[21] On the personal and human element in the play, see Morsbach, *Cäsarbild*, p. 29. As L. C. Knights recently emphasized, " it is the intolerable divorce between public life and the trust, loyalty and affection that men look for in personal living that explains the barrenness of action that is purely public and political " (" Shakespeare and Political Wisdom ", *Sewanee Rev.*, LXI (1953), 48).

[22] As Moulton puts it, " we get a supernatural foreshadowing of the end in the appearance to Brutus of Caesar's Ghost, and the omen Cassius sees . . . this lends the authority of the invisible world to our sense that the conspirators' cause is doomed. . . . The last remnant of justification for their cause ceases as the conspirators themselves seem to acknowledge their error and fate " (*Shakespeare as a Dramatic Artist*, p. 201).

[23] *Caesar*, p. xxxiii.

[24] *King John*, IV, ii, 104-105. The tragedy of Brutus, as can hardly be over-emphasized, is heightened by his ultimately realizing (if perhaps half-consciously only) that there is indeed no sure foundation

set on blood, and that his own blood only, which he is about to shed, can fully pay the ransom for Caesar's blood. This at least seems to be the deep meaning of his dying words, " Caesar, now be still." Here again the human element cannot be separated from the political issue, and this element it is which gives the fall of Brutus its real perspective and depth. Otherwise his tragedy might well have been reduced to that of an unsuccessful struggle against Caesarism, or the spirit of tyranny. Viewed strictly on the political plane, the disastrous result of the conspirators' deed, if it proves that they were mistaken, does not necessarily mean a definite verdict against them : it may simply indicate that they failed because Caesarism was the destiny of Rome; so that Casesar might have been the real tyrant in Shakespeare without its substantially altering the course of political events. This all the more since rebellion also happened to be condemned " even against manifest tyrants." Not so, however, on the human plane.

In a recent and timely lecture, Roy Walker also emphasizes Shakespeare's presentation of Caesar's killing as a crime against nature : " The fault, as Cassius had earlier told Brutus, is not in our stars but in ourselves, and nowadays we jump to the wrong conclusion about those too familiar lines. With biting tragic irony Shakespeare tells us that the fault is indeed not in the stars. . . . The fault is in Cassius. It is fatal to him and to Brutus, who allows himself to be tricked into the murder of the man who, whatever his human failings in age and health, never let his affections sway ' more than his reason '," and the critic rightly concludes that " the unselfish idealism of Brutus too has been against nature " (" The Northern Star : An Essay on the Roman Plays ", *SQ*, II, 1951, 289, 290).

King James' words, by the way, would provide a singularly pertinent comment on the political issue in the play : " Next, in place of relieving the commonwealth out of distresse (which is their onely excuse and colour) they shall heape double distresse and desolation upon it ; and so their rebellion shall procure the contrary effects that they pretend it for." (Quoted from *The Trew Law of Free Monarchies* by Muir, *Macbeth*, p. lxvii).

[25] And mark how conspicuous is the absence here, in Antony's monologue, of any allusion to the political motives of the crime.

[26] " The Problem of Time in *Julius Caesar*", *HLQ*, XIII (1950), 399-405. The following quotation is from p. 400.

[27] Dover Wilson, *Caesar*, p. xxxi.

[28] In opposition to Dover Wilson's view we may quote Professor Charlton : " Killing, surely, needs more excuse than this ; and Brutus' murder of Caesar is a killing which excites faint or overt suspicions of murder, patricide and regicide linked in one dread deed " (*Shakespearian Tragedy*, Cambridge, 1948, p. 77). One of the best formulations, however, was already given by Moulton half a century ago : " Brutus's own conscience being judge, the man against whom

he moves is guiltless ; and so the conscious sacrifice of justice and friendship to policy is a fatal error which is source sufficient for the whole tragedy of which Brutus is the hero " (*Shakespeare as a Dramatic Artist*, p. 176). See also A. Harbage, *As They Liked It. An Essay on Shakespeare and Morality* (New York, 1947), p. 85.

[29] See *Shakespeare Survey*, V (Cambridge, 1952), p. 129.

[30] " Or else this were a savage spectacle," *PMLA*, LXVI (1951), 765-766. On this point Brents Stirling has been slightly anticipated by John Palmer, who actually referred to " a blood rite " and to " the sacrificial mood in which Brutus struck the fatal blow ", without, however, examining the implications of the ritual. See *Political Characters of Shakespeare* (London, 1945), p. 14.

[31] *Op. cit.*, 769.

[32] *Ibid.*, 769-770. In another work, Professor Stirling writes that the speech " has the laconic and functional sparseness of the Gettysburg Address. Tragically, however, it is not delivered as a tribute to men who died in battle, but as a justification of a political *coup* and as an appeal for mass support " (*The Populace in Shakespeare*, New York, 1949, p. 29). The best appreciation, however, of the dramatic function of the speech is to be found in Maria Wickert's study : " Eine wirkungslose oder misslungene Brutusrede hätte die Peripetie unmittelbar auf Cäsars Ermordung folgen lassen und dadurch die Brutushandlung erstickt, noch ehe sie zur vollen Entfaltung gekommen war. Denn ihr positiver Gehalt, den Brutus mit dem Worte *redress* umschreibt, bliebe unentwickelt. Nun aber hat Shakespeare Brutus auf die volle Höhe des Erfolges geführt und ihn für einen kurzen Augenblick auf die Spitze des Staates gestellt, damit sein tragischer Absturz um so erschütternder wirke ; das Volk liess er durch die Abkehr von Cäsar als dem ihm gesetzten Herrscher mitschuldig werden, damit die Rache des Himmels das ganze Reich in ein Chaos stürzen konnte " (*op. cit.*, 24).

The contrary opinion probably found its most vigorous expression in Palmer's essay, who stressed that the speech served to emphasize " the political ineptitude of Brutus ", thought it " much to the credit of the Roman citizens that they listened attentively to this remarkable exercise in dialectic ", and claimed that it " had more success than it deserved " (*Political Characters*, pp. 23-24).

[33] It is of some interest to observe that each character in the political quartet in turn makes a similar kind of theatrical gesture implying the sacrifice of his own life : to top his refusal of the crown, Caesar offers the Roman mob his throat to cut ; Brutus shows the same people that he has a dagger ready for himself, in case Rome should need his death ; with half-hidden irony, Antony begs his death of the conspirators, and in the quarrel scene, Cassius gives his " naked breast " for Brutus to strike.

[34] Stauffer, *Shakespeare's World of Images*, p. 113.

³⁵ If it had not been for that one scene, Antony would have been the only character in the quartet constantly attracting our sympathies. We may suspect that it was partly in order not to show him *throughout* in a favourable light (and thus seriously jeopardize the balance in our sympathies) that Shakespeare introduced this short scene.

³⁶ O. J. Campbell, " The Salvation of Lear ", *ELH*, XV (1948), 95.

³⁷ The only exception occurs in l. 259, where the Folio reading is " Woe to the hand that shed this costly blood," and therefore seems to refer to (and single out) Brutus as against the other conspirators. I must acknowledge that this reading proved a little troublesome for my point here, jarring as it was with the significant plurals used by Antony in the scene (" your purpled hands " 159 ; " your hands " 219 ; " these butchers " 256 ; " these bloody men " 295). When shaking hands with each of the conspirators in turn, Antony of course used the singular in his respective addresses ; but here, why should the malediction light especially on one hand (in that case it cannot be but Brutus's) when the whole trend of the monologue directed against " these butchers " precisely points to Antony cursing the conspirators as a group and making no discrimination between them? Could it be that " the hand " was here used abstractedly, as a collective term for all the conspirators' bloody hands? In fact, the simplest way out— though a little too smooth and comfortable to be entirely satisfying— is to adopt R. G. White's emendation " Woe to the hands " (cf. Furness, *Caesar*, p. 159). That this emendation has recently been endorsed by so authoritative an expert on the Folio text as Dover Wilson (*Caesar*, pp. 51, 157) certainly speaks in favour of that rather handy solution.

³⁸ The contrast between Antony's deliberate indiscrimination and Brutus's decision to limit drastic measures to Caesar only, is subtly underlined by Cassius's brief reminder of (and regrets at) the sparing of Antony :

> Now, Brutus, thank yourself :
> This tongue had not offended so to-day,
> If Cassius might have ruled.
> (V. i. 45-47)

³⁹ Failure to understand the full implications of Antony's striking change of attitude towards Brutus, led B. R. Breyer to interpret Antony's final tribute as a piece of pure irony : " Even more ironic, perhaps, is the most celebrated speech of all, the ' noblest Roman ' speech. It is spoken of a man whom the same speaker only a hundred or so lines back has called to his face a hound, a flatterer and a traitor. And it is spoken in all earnestness ; the characters themselves seem unaware of these discrepancies between the outer and the inner Roman" ("A New Look at *Julius Caesar*", *Essays in Honor of Walter Clyde Curry*, Nashville, 1954, p. 179). The discrepancy, or rather the

reversal in Antony's attitude, is not meant to be ironic. The fact that Antony's mission is now successfully fulfilled, and that Brutus's death in the high Roman fashion has made up for Caesar's blood, makes all the difference.

[40] A touch which is conspicuously missing in the case of Richard III or Macbeth, whereas we have it again with Hamlet and Coriolanus, in the form of a funeral march.

[41] This " imaginative power to live fully in conflicting worlds " recently prompted Professor Stauffer to call Shakespeare " an Isaac Newton for human emotions ", who discovered the law : " For every action there is an equal and opposite reaction. Every emotion creates differing or supplementary or opposed emotions, and cannot be fully understood or described without them. Each decision, each course of conduct, generates the possibilities of other decisions and other courses " (*Shakespeare's World of Images*, p. 111). This directly leads us to one general aspect of Shakespeare's moral attitude as stressed by Professor Harbage : " Usually his method is to leave the issue undecided, to suspend or dissolve it, or to place the problem where we glimpse it only from the corner of our eye. Gazing at it directly must be an act of volition on our part. Any deciding vote on the rights of the case must be ours, not his " (*As They Liked It*, p. 84).

[42] Dover Wilson, *Caesar*, p. xxxii.

II

THE STRUCTURAL ROLE OF MOTIVES

But such simplicity in the over-all structure of that " streamlined drama " is of course not the whole story, and a different approach will gradually disclose that its antithetical balance rests on surprisingly rich and complex architectural patterns. So that *Julius Caesar* is simple only in the sense in which a cathedral could be called simple, because a bird's eye view of its outline may reveal the plain symmetry of a cross.

Indeed, " the simplicity of *Julius Caesar* is a surface simplicity only. To close analysis it reveals subtleties and complexities which render interpretation difficult."[1] But once the significance of the antithetical balance has been fully grasped, a good many of those subtleties and complexities become less difficult and can be interpreted as so many architectural patterns whose conjoined effects artistically enhance the bold sweep of the main structure. In other words, there is a group of motives subordinated to the main theme in such a way as to lend it greater depth and fulness of life, while closely fitted into the antithetical theme : their structural role is thus functional as much as pictorial. Inversely, their close connection with the very sense and sweep of the main theme gives them deeper perspective and greater significance.

It is to the study of that mutual and highly artistic relationship that we now wish to turn.

* * *

Superstition

> *As harbingers preceding still the fates*
> *And prologue to the omen coming on*

" No mob could be more abjectly servile than was that of Rome to the superstition of portents, prodigies, and omens."[2] Such disdainful comment on a long past and absurd credulity—the immeasurable superiority of an enlightened age being tacitly assumed—is typical of a current attitude towards manifestations of the primitive mind. And the more so, since the stricture was pronounced not by some spare and extra-dry rationalist, but by a man who had drunk of poppies and mandragora, and whose mind had been haunted by the rich and alluring phantasms of *paradis artificiels.*

In fact, we are so spontaneously inclined to look upon belief in premonitory signs with a self-complacent disdain or, at best, mild condescension, that it threatens to distort our judgment when we come to deal with the problem of Caesar's superstition. It is manifest enough that we automatically consider it as a testimony of sheer weakness on the hero's part, deliberately introduced and emphasized by Shakespeare.

Thus—to quote but two modern critics—Dover Wilson, expatiating on Shakespeare's caustic portrait of Caesar, includes superstition as one of the outstanding traits building up the " contemptible side of the character " which, he adds, " is solely of his own making."[3] While Mr. Stewart points out that if Shakespeare, on the one hand, " modifies Plutarch to give Caesar a more striking nobility, magnanimity," on the other, he also modifies him " to give Caesar more of infirmity, both bodily and spiritual," so much so that " in Plutarch we are told that Calpurnia had not formerly been superstitious but was become so, but in Shakespeare this is transferred to Caesar :

> he is Superstitious growne of late,
> Quite from the maine Opinion he held once."[4]

It is clear that both the Lupercal incident and the matter of the omens are thus put under the same heading and, instanced as sheer examples of Caesarian superstition, exclusively considered under their shady aspect. To pretend that such views are wrong would be pushing the limits of paradox to absurdity. Yet we do not think it too wildly extravagant to suggest that Caesar's superstition is not purely negative, not all-of-a-piece, but on the contrary, like many another feature in that supremely dualistic play, subtly ambivalent.

For clearness we shall first deal with the question of portents and premonitory dreams, then with the Lupercal incident. That Caesar's superstition is ambivalent is already suggested by the first two instances which serve as a touchstone for it. The curious belief in the virtue of the racer's touch to cure sterility, since it provides us with an example of crass superstition, by itself alone straightforwardly testifies to a striking amount of credulity on Caesar's part. But this is the first impression only. The next, and immediately following instance stands in apparently full contradiction with it. When the soothsayer's shrill cries finally reach Caesar's " good " ear, and urge him to beware the ides of March, he dismisses him as a dreamer.

The contrast is so glaring indeed, that three-quarters of a century ago, already, a German critic endeavoured to explain it by maintaining that Shakespeare's Caesar was not meant to be superstitious : " It has been thought that Caesar here shows himself childishly superstitious. . . . But what Shakespeare wishes clearly to indicate is Caesar's anxiety for an heir to his power and the establishing of a dynasty. That he was not actually superstitious is shown shortly after by his curt dismissal of the soothsayer."[5] Yet, as we shall presently see, the contrast goes deeper and is susceptible of a better explanation. But let us turn to the omens.

Both in the plays written not very long before and after *Julius Caesar*, we have important references to the belief in the monitory purport of natural prodigies. And what is more, Shakespeare uses the motive neither flippantly, nor with his tongue in his cheek, but quite earnestly, with a set dramatic purpose. Even if we limit ourselves to *Hamlet* and *King John*, the parallels are significant enough. Just as the soothsayer in *Julius Caesar* eventually proved right, so did Peter of Pomfret, the soothsayer in *King John*. With the one difference, however, that while Caesar was only warned against the ides of March with no actual prediction formulated (so that the threat involved was thoroughly vague), the prophet of Pomfret not only announced the exact date, but the very hour on which John would have to relinquish the crown, " foreknowing that the truth will fall out so." This may well explain, partly at least, the difference between John's and Caesar's reactions. First of all, and curiously enough, the very same word rises to their lips :

> *King John :* Thou idle dreamer   (IV. ii. 153)
> *Caesar :* He is a dreamer ;   (I. ii. 24)

and the word is fraught with greater significance in Caesar's mouth.[6] But there the analogy ceases, and the contrast is all to Caesar's advantage : " let us leave him : pass." This sober restraint implies a full mastery over his nerves, an equanimity which is conspicuously missing in the overstrained and impulsive usurper. Listen to John :

> away with him ; imprison him ;
> And on that day at noon, whereon he says
> I shall yield up my crown, let him be hang'd.
> (IV. ii. 155-7)

Majesty and aloofness have given way to vindictive wrath. Now

Peter's prophecy is but one item in the dreadful roll of dismal tidings which suddenly sweep down on the hapless king. No sooner has the prophet been taken away, and John further acquainted with the rebellion of the nobles, than Hubert announces the startling apparition of the five moons :

> Four fixed, and the fifth did whirl about
> The other four in wondrous motion.
>   *King John :* Five moons!
>   *Hubert :* Old men and beldams in the streets
> Do prophesy upon it dangerously :
> Young Arthur's death is common in their mouths.
>   (IV. ii. 183-7)

Thus a natural prodigy accompanies the death of Arthur, the legitimate heir, which was yet unknown since Hubert had eventually spared him.

The dramatic implications of the point are clear. The disastrous news that assault the king are felt to be consequences of his criminal order. Such a violent breach of the natural law has brought disruption within the kingdom, and this disruption in its turn tears into the integrity of the King's own microcosm. Deeply does he now repent his deed :

> Nay, in the body of this fleshly land,
> This kingdom, this confine of blood and breath,
> Hostility and civil tumult reigns
> Between my conscience and my cousin's death.
>   (IV. ii. 245-8)

The elements themselves reflect the disorder thereby created in the regular course of Nature, and are thus " shaken into a common sympathy " with the premature and unnatural death of the poor sovereign-child.

Such correspondences, though partly based on irrational features, are powerfully suggestive and poetically conceived, and it is undeniable that Shakespeare achieved a fine dramatic effect when skilfully including the motive as part of a greater pattern. But we can only be really touched if we respond imaginatively and not through the narrow channel of the discursive mind.

This is confirmed by *Hamlet* which is of especial interest here since the reference is to the very omens that preceded the fall of Caesar. And, once more, the circumstances are such as bear witness to a serious and dramatic use of the motive. Horatio's vivid description of the portents serves a double purpose. When still startled by his first glimpse of the portentous figure so like the king that's dead, Horatio has an inkling that it " bodes some strange eruption to our state." This shows a sudden change in his attitude as he had been sceptical before the actual appearance of the ghost. But then, the expository talk about the warlike preparations against young Fortinbras, almost an anticlimax, gives him time to shake off his sombre forebodings and, recovering his balance, the philosopher and scholar " belittles the Ghost ; the apparition, he says, is nothing to what happened before Caesar's death or to more recent portents."[7] But if this parallel shows us a Horatio intent upon belittling the Ghost, it also makes us aware of how much he has been shaken by the apparition, since he must try and quell his own weird misgivings by appealing to a much greater calamity : the classical example of one of the most spectacular downfalls in history. All this makes us still more receptive to the disquieting element in the mysterious apparition. And the reference to the omens cannot be laughed (or spirited) away without destroying the atmosphere of the whole passage. " As in *Julius Caesar* and *King Lear* "—Professor Stoll is writing on *Macbeth*—" Nature undergoes an upheaval, both portending and accompanying, in virtue of a superstition not then extinct, the fall of the monarch."[8]

Now the question which is likely to be asked is this : do you actually suggest that Shakespeare believed in that superstition? We might as well ask whether he believed in ghosts, or in magic, or in the immortality of the soul, or in reincarnation for that matter.[9] Such questions are absolutely beside the point (not to mention that they are objectively unanswerable). What matters is Shakespeare's intuitive grasp of the associational powers of a given belief, or notion—what we might call its potent valences— allowing him to achieve its complete transposition to the level of dramatic art. And it here appears that the rich possibilities of the present motive have been used in accordance with the artistic requirements of poetic drama.

That this should further imply Shakespeare's instinctive aware- ness of a collective subconscious mind, almost in the Jungian sense of the word, no longer makes us gasp, even if it rasps our rational fibre. In one of the many illuminating passages of his study, Mr. Stewart stresses that " what is really significant is the sort of awareness for which Shakespeare wrote. The awareness of an audience settled in a theatre is not that of a reader over his

book. It is substantially a group awareness ; there is a merging
of consciousness ; doors are thrown open which even the practised reader can never hope to do more than push slightly ajar."[10]
Now this group awareness, this merging of consciousness
necessarily tends to work away from the curbs and strictures of
logic and reason, and favour a much greater receptivity towards
the appeal of irrational voices from the depths, which are then
much more audible and operative.

As a rule, Shakespeare could thus rely even on most of the
thinking people (if not perhaps all disciples of Reginald Scott) to
be led into a temporary suspension of disbelief, or scepticism, in
omens, prophecies and other superstitions, and rendered as it
were collectively and emotionally receptive to the appeal of such
notions in their dramatic context.[11] And this even apart from what
has been termed the " mildly hypnogenic " effect of great poetry.
In other words, the kind of scepticism we find in Horatio probably
reflects that of part of the cultivated audience ; and we may well
suppose that when he drops it under the impact of the awe-
inspiring vision, group awareness also induced even the most
fastidious spectators to react with him and unconsciously tune
in to the perceptible whisper of ancestral voices prophesying
war and strange eruptions in the state![12]

To those who are suspicious of the use of analytical psychology
in Shakespearean criticism, there are simpler arguments to
advance. That Caesar's superstition is not to be taken as sheer
weakness is also suggested by the attitude of his adversaries at
the time of the conspiracy. It is characteristic that Casca, for one,
who was so ready to poke fun at ceremonies, and whose mocking
narrative hardly betrayed any ingrafted reverence and awe is so
much impressed, in the very next scene, by the tempestuous night
and its weird pageant of prodigies, that he is awed into a supernatural interpretation :

> When these prodigies
> Do so conjointly meet, let not men say
> ' These are their reasons : they are natural :'
> For, I believe, they are portentous things
> Unto the climate that they point upon.
> (I. iii. 28-32)

And that is why, when in a further scene, reference is made to
Caesar having lately grown superstitious, Casca keeps singularly
silent, whereas we might have otherwise expected at least a drop

of sour humour, if not a jeering cascade of jibes.

Even Cassius, who has launched the bitterest attacks against Caesar, angrily referring to him as " so vile a thing as Caesar," mentions the latter's recent superstitious tendencies with a lack of passion, nay, an objectivity which is rather surprising in a man only too prone to charge him with contemptible faults. And this all the more since Cassius, unlike Casca, far from looking pale with fear, or casting himself in wonder

> To see the strange impatience of the heavens,

enjoyed the perilous night and bared his bosom to the thunder-stone : as he acknowledges later, he certainly held Epicurus strong.[13]

Thus, there is no single instance in the play where the super-stitious element is ridiculed or written down. Even at its worst, when dealt with by a sceptic like Cassius, it remains an open question.

Contrasting the stately appearance of Caesar and his train, and the high expectations of all spectators, with the first words we hear from his mouth, Palmer ironically comments : " All Rome is bent to hear this Caesar. O lame and impotent conclusion! The first words that fall from his lips show faith in an old wives' tale. Caesar is himself half-ashamed of his credulity. The belief that Calpurnia's sterility can be cured by the touch of a runner in the feast of Lupercal he attributes, not to himself, but to ' our elders '."[14] But the comment is scarcely justified, for it is only the modern reader who, unlike the deadly foes of Caesar—not to speak of his friends and followers—considers the belief with derision. But Shakespeare does not mean us to look upon it with derision, and nowhere do we find the remotest intention to disclose what has been called " the base machinery of ropes and pulleys, which sustained the miserable jugglery played off upon the popular credulity."[15]

If representatives of both contending parties in turn attack specific ceremonies or rituals practised by their adversaries (as has been evinced by Professor Stirling), those often insidious, biting, or devastating assaults leave superstitions conspicuously un-scathed. Thus is Antony's threefold offering of the crown abundantly scoffed at by Casca, while Caesar's order to the same Antony to touch Calpurnia " in this holy chase " which might have provided excellent stuff for mocking a superstitious dictator, athirst for an heir, is completely ignored.[16]

If we have dwelt at some length on the whole point, it is because the common assumption that the motive of superstition merely illustrates a weakness in Caesar does but lamely account for its actual significance, which must be sought elsewhere. What strikes us is the outstanding difference in Caesar's attitude, according to the underlying trend of a given superstition. He is only inclined to trust in the significance of premonitory signs, or the value of superstitious beliefs, in so far as they do involve a favourable outcome. Thus, he waves aside the soothsayer's warning, pronouncing the prophet a dreamer, because the *mise en garde* implies a negative element : it means at the very least a threatening danger which might well jeopardize Caesar within reach of his goal, on the road to final success. On the other hand, though he is not quite sure of its operative power, he feels rather disposed to believe in the curative virtue of the runner's touch because, should it work as the elders maintain, it would answer his own wishes. It is, if we may put it so, as if his own wishes were, in a way, father to the credulous thought. And we therefore doubt that Caesar is " half-ashamed " of his credulity : he is rather half-consciously tempted to believe in the superstition because there lurks the secret promise of fulfilment.

Again, he systematically wants to ignore the heaped-up testimonies of the nightly portents, of Calpurnia's prophetic dream and of the augurs' *caveat* because all tend to a conclusion unfavourable for him. And what he wants from the augurs is a propitious verdict :

> Go bid the priests do present sacrifice,
> And bring me their opinions of success.
>
> (II. ii. 5-6)

In that case he would believe them sure enough. But when the oracle is negative, he at once rebels and defies it : " Caesar shall go forth." The dire portents of the stormy night are so obvious and so palpable to anybody that he cannot simply wave them aside, but he evades them by pronouncing them valid for everybody as well as himself :

> these predictions
> Are to the world in general as to Caesar.
>
> (II. ii. 28-9)

Yet the finest illustration comes with Calpurnia's dream. In a piece of sound enough *Traumdeutung*, Calpurnia immediately sees through the symbolism of her striking dream and, in a prophetic strain, interprets the image in terms of evils imminent. But this again is not palatable to Caesar. Though he feels that there is something in it—what with the corroborative evidence of the priests and the storm—he is not at all convinced : " these does *she* apply for warnings and portents." He only yields because, he says, Calpurnia

<blockquote>
on her knee
Hath begg'd that I will stay at home to-day.
(II. ii. 81-2)
</blockquote>

How sudden the shift as soon as Decius offers a favourable interpretation. If Calpurnia's Cassandrian warnings were distasteful to Caesar, now Decius' words ' expounding ' the dream into a vision fair and fortunate, immediately appeal to him. Mark how eagerly he snatches at them:

<blockquote>
How foolish do your fears seem now, Calpurnia!
I am ashamed I did yield to them.
Give me my robe, for I will go.
(II. ii. 105-7)
</blockquote>

This throws a different light on the much scoffed at dialogue with his wife. " Caesar has declared himself immovable. But Calpurnia, knowing her lord, offers him a way out and the natural man grasps it with an eagerness which shows how empty were the protestations of the demigod. ' Call it *my* fear that keeps you in the house ', suggests the tactful wife, and Caesar complies immediately."[17] Palmer, we think, let himself be carried off his feet by his humorous twist. As we have already emphasized, Caesar only complies after his wife has thrown herself down on her knees, and we must here again point out how Shakespeare subtly conveyed the simple human touch lying behind Caesar's acceptance, by the sudden transition from the third person to the first. Far from being empty, the protestations, we now realize, spring from a deeper source : Caesar's instinctive reluctance to believe in anything but favourable portents and a favourable outcome.[18]

This attitude, we suggest, illustrates one aspect of the ineradicable trust in one's own star, without which no great military or political figure can ever hope to reach complete prominence. That this somewhat irrational faith does sometimes happen to precipitate the very downfall of the great man himself, is but a striking instance of how close the Tarpeian rock stands to the

Capitol, and how unstable the wheel of Fortune. There comes a moment, indeed, when an enormous risk must be taken in the course of one's life. As Brutus himself is to say :

> There is a tide in the affairs of men
> Which taken at the flood leads on to fortune ;
> Omitted, all the voyage of their life
> Is bound in shallows and in miseries.
>
> (IV. iii. 215-9)

Brutus takes the risk, too, and it leads him to disaster. Rightly or wrongly, Caesar feels that if he gives up going to the Senate, the opportunity for final success will be for ever lost. In spite of ill-omens, he cannot abandon faith in his own destiny without losing faith in himself. Should we then simply see therein, with Dover Wilson, the image of a Caesar stalking " blindly to his doom?" Since time immemorial, no doubt, gods have been suspected to blind the unlucky mortals whom they wanted to destroy. But this may be only one half of the picture, and perhaps we should also see therein, with De Quincey, an illustration of " the unusual force of mind, and the heroic will, which obstinately laid aside these concurring prefigurations of impending destruction."[19]

Moreover, this impending destruction, the possibility of which Caesar ignored, was to be achieved by crime, by a highly unnatural deed involving at the same time the transgression of the sacred law of love and friendship. That much is implied in his last words, at the sight of Brutus's dagger : " then fall Caesar." That his own precious friend should have so far betrayed his trust as to secretly join his enemies and assassins, shatters Caesar's world which is no longer worth living in. Danger Caesar can look in the face, but when the loyalty of a man like Brutus fails, then he hides his own face, then cracks his noble heart : everything collapses, the natural order of things has turned to topsy-turvydom. Thus Caesar, who refused to believe in portents which did not spell success because he had full faith in his own star, who deliberately discarded the dangers ready to assail him on his way to a supreme achievement, who thought himself beyond aggression, now offers no resistance and silently resigns himself to die.

Here we may pause awhile, the better to realize how brilliantly the motive of superstition is woven into the great antithetical structure of the play. For the theme is taken over again after

Caesar's death—though for a time it looks as if it had entirely vanished out of the picture. And when it reappears, just before Philippi, it takes on new significance. It is as if Caesar's death had caused strange mutations in the spirit of the main conspirators. To Cassius, we remember, there was no ambivalence in Caesar's superstition : for him, though he did not apparently charge it as a weakness, Caesar had definitely turned superstitious; and if Cassius, who was only too prone to malign Caesar, mentioned the point as a bare fact, with no actual blame involved, it is because such superstition was spontaneously shared by some of his own friends like Casca or Cinna. But one point which clearly emerges from his dialogue with Casca is that Cassius himself was free from the general superstition and prided himself on being immune from the fears of the dreadful night. As for Brutus, his stoicism by itself would prevent him from being impressed by the disturbed sky into a foreboding mood. His Aurelian poise Shakespeare subtly conveys in a brief picture. Opposed to Casca's, Cinna's, or even Cassius' reactions[20] is Brutus's unshakable attitude : with him the elements—" the unaccustom'd terror of this night "—are only referred to incidentally, almost parenthetically, and with a complete absence of emotional strain :

> The exhalations whizzing in the air
> Give so much light that I may read by them.
>
> (II. i. 44-5)

It is a little as if one should say, so bright does the moon shine tonight that I can read my paper.

Now Cassius is suddenly " shaken out of his philosophical scepticism by the portents which appeared upon the march to Philippi,"[21] and goes as far as to say that he has changed his mind and partly credits things that do presage, so that, coming from Sardis, the birds' shadows

> seem
> A canopy *most fatal*, under which
> Our army lies, ready to give up the ghost.
>
> (V. i. 86-8)

In other words he followed exactly the same evolution as that with which he previously credited Caesar who, in Cassius's own words, was

> superstitious grown of late,
> Quite from the main opinion he held once

> Of fantasy, of dreams and ceremonies.
>
> (II. i. 195-7)

Brutus, on the other hand, who remained so stoically (and naturally) unperturbed by all the fires and the gliding ghosts appearing in the fearful night before the Ides of March, is now convinced that the apparition of Caesar's ghost bodes strange eruptions to himself and his own cause :

> The ghost of Caesar hath appear'd to me
> Two several times by night ; at Sardis once,
> And this last night here in Philippi fields :
> I know my hour is come.
>
> (V. v. 17-20)

Thus Sardis, in a way, is a Damascus both to Brutus and to Cassius.[22] Their strangely parallel evolution is an unmistakable spiritual premonition of Caesar's imminent revenge, a sign that his mighty spirit, walking abroad, has now finally shaken the two main conspirators' minds out of their assurance : they who so far implicitly defied augury, are made aware that in consequence of their action destiny has now turned against them. The dramatic effect of that striking reversal is finally heightened by the profound irony implied in the situation. Caesar did not ultimately believe in the unfavourable omens—and was wrong. Brutus and Cassius ultimately believed in them—and were right. And whereas Caesar was willing to die (hiding his face in his mantle) because Brutus had made his world out of joint, Brutus himself willingly died, thereby setting it right again.

To conclude, the motive throbs in what might be called a systolic rhythm, and its two complementary movements thus stand in close and harmonical correlation with the pulse of the main theme. In such correspondences, both simple and subtle, may well lurk one secret of the fine artistry which lends the drama its beautiful finish.

Suicide

A similar artistic relevance can be found in the motive of suicide, the evolution of which is of the highest interest and well worth tracing from the first statement of the theme to the final climax of Brutus's self-destruction.

What underlies the treatment of the theme and gives it full significance is the use of tragic irony—here a sharp and penetrating instrument which exhibits the governing hand of fate, and ultimately reveals the very core of the whole drama.

For clearness we shall first examine the motive with reference to Cassius, then turn to Brutus, without however losing sight of the close connection between the two aspects of the theme. Besides, what Shakespeare retains from, modifies in, or adds to, Plutarch must of course be constantly kept in mind.

There are indeed two divergences from Plutarch in the presentation of Cassius's suicide which, trivial as they may seem, turn out to be of no mean importance for an assessment of the full implications of the motive.

The first consists in Shakespeare's addition of three " meditative lines", uttered by Cassius, which are no less than a direct premonition of his own imminent end :

> This day I breathed first : time is come round,
> And where I did begin, there shall I end ;
> My life is run his compass.
>
> (V. v. 23-25)

As Dover Wilson points out, they serve the immediate stage purpose of allowing the Pindarus actor " just time to exit at one of the side-doors and climb the hidden stair to the upper stage."[23] But behind that neat little device loom larger issues. Had Shakespeare put the passage but half a dozen lines after, there would have been nothing peculiar or striking about it. As it stands, it means that before he knows the result of Titinius' mission—which might alter, and actually could have altered, the whole solution in a decisive way—without even waiting for the assurance " whether yond troups are friend or enemy," which makes all the difference, Cassius has given up the struggle and knows that his death is at hand. Whether the presentiment arises from the coincidence of that decisive action falling on his birthday —and therefore a time particularly apt to mark that his wheel of life had come full circle—or from a deeper intuition is immaterial. Shakespeare thereby successfully conveys that his Cassius is morally defeated before the last fateful stroke. And this is but the final term of a gradation which develops in the second part of the drama.

For this moral collapse is no sudden crisis. It is the outcome of a slow disintegration which began with the quarrel scene (" For Cassius is aweary of the world "), found ominous expression in the change of mind which led him partly to believe

in a fatal presage, could be sensed behind the dialogue with
Brutus where Cassius, despite some optimistic declarations, felt
urged to " reason with the worst that might befall," and now
reaches its apex. That this disintegration is a far-reaching
consequence of Caesar's murder is undoubtful. For much more
than in Plutarch we have been made aware of a deep irony in
Cassius's death.

Let us turn to his first statement about suicide. Emotionally
we cannot but approve of Cassius, for the statement is set in
terms of an opposition between liberty and tyranny, emphatically
asserting the primacy of the spirit over the material aspect of
tyrannical oppression. Should Caesar wear a crown, says Cassius,

> I know where I will wear this dagger then :
> Cassius from bondage will deliver Cassius.
> Therein, ye gods, you make the weak most strong ;
> Therein, ye gods, you tyrants do defeat :
> Nor stony tower, nor walls of beaten brass,
> Nor airless dungeon, nor strong links of iron,
> Can be retentive to the strength of spirit ;
> But life, being weary of these worldly bars,
> Never lacks power to dismiss itself.
>
> (I. iii. 89-97)

There is no conflict, no questioning whether 'tis nobler to suffer
tyranny—the point is settled, the resolve is firm : " I know. . . ."
In this proud context, indeed, the catchword death rather than
bondage has much to commend itself, especially as we feel that
Cassius really means it. How seriously, we are soon to know at
the dramatic moment when it looks as if the whole plot had
suddenly been revealed to Caesar, and the conspirators' action
seems on the verge of an irremediable collapse. Cassius does not
waver, he is immediately resolved to die :

> If this be known,
> Cassius or Caesar never shall turn back,
> For I will slay myself.
>
> (III. i. 20-22)

Nor should we dismiss this by simply pointing out that Shakespeare found the incident in his source. For in Plutarch, " all
were of a mind that it was no tarrying for them till they were
apprehended, but rather that they should kill themselves with
their own hands."[24] Shakespeare singles out Cassius only for
that purpose. So far, this side of Cassius—his stern adherence

to the high Roman fashion—is entirely positive. Suppose the plot had been discovered and he had actually killed himself before he was arrested, there is hardly any doubt that the audience would have judged him (despite his faults) as a noble victim dying for the cause of liberty.

But this is before the murder. Afterwards, something is amiss with Cassius. And his will not be after all quite that sort of proud death he had formerly contemplated and was resolved upon. For he did not leave betimes—he left too early. Spiritually shaken, yet resigned (his meditative lines prove it), " mistrust of good success " was much too readily assumed. And thus it was decreed that he should kill himself not so much because there was no other way to escape from bondage, but ironically enough, because he had, in his own friend's words " misconstrued everything!" Viewed in that light there may well be some further irony implied in his outcry about the cowardly ensign whom he had just slain:

> Myself have to mine own turn'd enemy.
> (V. iii. 2)

Are we not likely to realize in a brief flash that Cassius's words are doubly true, for he actually turned enemy to his own much earlier, when stabbing Caesar? His dying recognition that with his suicide Caesar is revenged—Shakespeare's addition to Plutarch—effectively connects the irony of his death with the initial murder of which it is, in a way, a consequence willed by destiny itself.

" Alas, thou hast misconstrued everything!" exclaims Titinius at the sight of Cassius's body. True enough. Yet if we turn to the second modification from Plutarch which we want to emphasize, it will be seen that Shakespeare stressed the part played by destiny in the fall of Cassius. For what Titinius did not know, and could not know, is that the " hateful error " did not actually spring from Cassius. In Plutarch, as will be remembered, the mistake is entirely due to Cassius himself. The shouts of joy and songs of victory of Brutus's horsemen on meeting Titinius "marred all. For Cassius, thinking indeed that Titinius was taken of the enemies ", went back to his tent and gave Pindarus " his head to be stricken off."[25] Now with Shakespeare it is Pindarus who is responsible for the error. Sent on reconnaissance by Cassius, he misinterprets the whole scene and reports from the hill : " He's ta'en. And, hark! they shout for joy " (V. iii. 32). So that Cassius *could not but misconstrue* the whole occurrence—as only the audience is aware. And a last echo of that tragic irony rings in the spectators' ears when brave Titinius, lamenting Cassius's death before he kills himself in his turn, cries to his friend's body " Didst thou not hear their shouts?" Today, indeed, the gods did not stand friendly, and Cassius's ominous intimation at Sardis eloquently proves true. The presage did not lie which meant that he and all his friends " were sickly prey."

The suicide motive has a similar import with reference to Brutus, though its treatment shows greater concentration ; and if somewhat more elusive perhaps, the tragic irony is none the less quite real. Commenting on Brutus's negative attitude towards suicide, as expressed in his last dialogue with Cassius, and the apparent contradiction it shows with his next speech and his own suicide, Dover Wilson refuses to see therein any inconsistency : " North makes Brut. say that though he disapproves of suicide in theory, ' being now in the midst of danger, I am of a contrary mind '; Sh. instead of reporting this change of opinion, shows it actually taking place : i.e. the philosopher condemns suicide . . . the Roman soldier, faced with the prospect of walking in Ant.'s triumph, sees in it the only honourable course."[26] The comment is of great interest. For if this interpretation holds good (and no serious reason seems to oppose it) this means that for the first time in the play Brutus is clearly led to contemplate acting himself in flagrant opposition to his own philosophical ideal, and this in a matter of capital importance. So far, Brutus had always endeavoured to act in accordance with his own idealistic principles. That was the basis of his honesty. That this occasion-ally involved him in serious tactical mistakes (which an adherence to Cassius's advice would have avoided) has already been evident enough. But the mistakes arose precisely from his belief in the superiority of his own ideal and ideas which was his *raison d'être*. Now confronted with the dread consequences of a possible defeat, he implicitly endorses Cassius's attitude and more or less tacitly admits that suicide is the only way out. His motive, namely that " he bears too great a mind " to go bound to Rome, im-perfectly conceals the deadlock to which his ideal of stoicism leads him when it clashes with what for him would be the harshest reality in this earthly life. To apply the tenets of stoicism strictly would finally result in a situation such as the very greatness of his mind could not endure. That Brutus does not see the irony makes it the greater for us.

But we have been somewhat prepared for this irony which in its turn leads us to a deeper one. His first slip—if we may call it so—is revealed in the quarrel scene where he encroaches upon his principle of strict justice in favour of Cassius, whose corruption ought to have been punished :

> The name of Cassius honours this corruption,
> And chastisement doth therefore hide his head.
>
> (IV. iii. 15-6)

That such a concession to an unpleasant reality threatens to undermine the solidity of Brutus's moral edifice, and to question retrospectively the very foundation on which the motives for killing Caesar were based, can be perceived in the violence of his outburst :

> Remember March, the ides of March remember :
> Did not Julius bleed for justice' sake?
> What villain touch'd his body, that did stab,
> And not for justice?
>
> (IV. iii. 18-21)

Indeed, what seems to be implied at bottom is that if Caesar was killed for justice' sake and his executioners themselves incapable of promoting justice, then the murder was done in vain. And this, of course, Brutus could never admit. None the less there is some uneasiness over the contradiction between his avowed principles of integrity and his demand for certain sums of gold which, " in such a time as this," could only be raised by vile and oppressive means. This ironical clash, however, does not directly involve Brutus's own actions, but it prepares us in a way for the greater irony inherent in the *impasse* to which his philosophy now leads him.

As Dover Wilson comments, Brutus " finds it no more possible to die by philosophy than to live by it in this rude world."[27] But the one thing he found possible to do by philosophy was to kill Caesar. Is that not perhaps the supreme irony of Brutus's life, and is this irony not reflected in the striking ambivalence of his condemnation of suicide, expressed in terms which retrospectively mean at the same time quite as definite (and devastating) a condemnation of his killing Caesar :[28]

> I do find it cowardly and vile,
> For fear of what might fall, so to prevent
> The time of life.
>
> (V. i. 103-5)

Was not the whole theoretical justification of his decision precisely based on what *might* happen *if* Caesar were crowned? Does this not lead us naturally to another deep irony lurking behind his last message to his countrymen :

> My heart doth joy that yet in all my life
> I found no man but he was true to me.
>
> (V. v. 34-5)

As Mr. Stewart puts it, " A Roman thought! But Caesar's last words had been ' Et tu, Brute —and uttering them he had muffled up his face and struggled no more."[29] One might tentatively see it as a sort of spiritual *mea culpa* (however unwittingly uttered), that on the very threshold of death Brutus should recognize as a supreme blessing that no man ever proved untrue to him : perhaps the unconscious equivalent, on the spiritual plane, of his dying recognition that his own blood makes up the audit for the blood of Caesar.[30]

One may possibly differ as to the meaning of the tragic irony. Professor Sewell concludes that " External events cast an ironical shadow over the honesty of Brutus, and we marvel that in such good could be mixed such evil . . . but it is no argument from failure that makes us question the earlier decision. . . . To find the flaw in this honesty in something particular to the act, making it dishonest, is to destroy the meaning of the play. For the study of Brutus is a study in that evil original in our flesh which brings in a little corruption—and often more than a little— whenever man, in decision and action, addresses himself, as he must, to his world."[31] This is sound and pertinent enough. Nevertheless, the ironical shadow is not only due to external events. A deeply ironical penumbra also finds its source within that " little kingdom " of Brutus, which is the " state of man."[32] And we again suggest that the insurrection which finally destroys it against its own laws ultimately derives not from a flaw in his honesty—there Professor Sewell is right—but from Brutus's transgression of a natural human law. No human being, even with the best theoretical motives, can possibly be condemned and executed for fear of what he may become. In spite of that evil original in his flesh, surely man can address himself to his world, however heavily burdened he is with a great responsibility, without necessarily transgressing that law. In other words it was an act committed against nature, for fear of what might fall so to prevent the time of life of Julius Caesar. There is enough irony, both external and internal, in Brutus's suicide to confirm that this was the price he paid for it.[33]

Sleep and Slumber

O soft embalmer of the still midnight!

Broadly speaking, the motives of superstition and suicide are drawn on the same lines as the general pattern of the main theme, inasmuch as the transformations they illustrate are subtly related to and conditioned by the great throbbing rhythm of the central action, and help to bring its full significance into focus. Thus the alterations which the murder of Caesar has brought about not only externally, in the fortunes of the main conspirators, but internally, in their very spirits, are vividly reflected in both motives.

But behind the spectacular and stirring reversals, the very substance of the whole tragedy, there is an unobtrusive little something which does not change. Great captains and rulers are precipitated from their pedestals, political systems are shattered, insurrections and upheavals make feverish the body of the state and that microcosm which is the state of man, the elements themselves seem shaken out of their natural order and anticipate the general turmoil—yet one frail and tiny thread remains unshaken, an almost imperceptible and incorporeal axis of stability : the sleep of a child, a symbol of innocence. As a delicate foil, that soothing element of continuity, by its rare contrast with the universal mutability and topsy-turvydom, brings it home more powerfully than many a catastrophe. Artistically this is a master stroke which seems to have escaped the search-lights of the critics.

" In Shakespeare, so far as I am acquainted with him, there are no such ' insoluble ' problems (as the Cornelian dilemmas for instance), such Hegelian antinomies—deadlocks or blind-alleys, and, besides, no technique that would do for dealing with them. . . . Brutus soliloquizing on the reasons for and against the assassination is (as everyone knows) quite unenlightening and unsatisfactory." So Professor Stoll in a recent review.[34] Apart from Brutus's relatively short soliloquy, the dilemma is not actually debated on the stage, and in that sense, Professor Stoll is right. But in that sense only. For we know that the dilemma tore into the harmony of Brutus's mind and deeply weighed on his whole behaviour before it led to the dreadful deed, and the Gordian knot was cut. Nor is this knowledge derived from unwarranted and flimsy speculations of the kind that have now been so long and sturdily fought out by the distinguished champion of the historical school. How long Brutus's inner conflict lasted, and how deep it was, are not questions beyond the boundaries of the stage or the play—as if one were to ask how many children had noble Portia. They are indirectly treated by Shakespeare himself, who depicts the effect of the dilemma on Brutus much more than Brutus's grappling with it; and for being emotionally suggested and answered rather than actually brought on the boards in eloquent Cornelian tirades, they are none the less real and vivid.

The first words we have from Brutus about himself already seem to give us a hint: " I am not gamesome." They may denote a general aspect of his character since he opposes the trait to Antony's "quick spirit", and have been so interpreted by critics. But they may also denote, more particularly, his present mood, the outcome of a recent development reflected in Cassius's reproach :

> I have not from your eyes that gentleness
> And show of love as I was wont to have.
>
> (I. ii. 34-5)

In any case it is soon obvious that we have before us a man suffering from an inner conflict—an unnamed conflict causing him to forget the shows of love to other men, as he himself acknowledges :

> if I have veil'd my look,
> I turn the trouble of my countenance
> Merely upon myself. Vexed I am
> Of late with passions of some difference,
> Conceptions only proper to myself,
> Which give some soil perhaps to my behaviours.
>
> (I. ii. 37-42)

There is no possible doubt, moreover, that the conflict arises from a deep dilemma—though we cannot yet quite fathom it—since he speaks of himself as " poor Brutus with himself at war." How gradually and subtly the source of the conflict is revealed to us, from Cassius's allusion that people " groaning underneath this age's yoke " do wish that " noble Brutus had his eyes " to Brutus's final decision (" It must be by his death "), is once more a masterpiece of Shakespearean exposition which needs no further comment here. What must be stressed, however, is that even after we have been acquainted with the dilemma and Brutus's solution, we have once more to realize by reflection, and half retrospectively, how deep the problem gnawed into his mind. That a man of Brutus's stamp should have been moved so much that his noble Portia (who does not yet know why) is led to complain :

> It will not let you eat, nor talk, nor sleep,
> And, could it work so much upon your shape
> As it hath much prevail'd on your condition,
> I should not know you, Brutus. . . .
>
> (II. i. 252-5)

is more eloquent perhaps—in any case more concrete—than a whole debate. " Nor sleep " . . . Indeed, what could have conveyed a better image of the intensity of Brutus's inner struggle than the lack of sleep?

As is so often the case with Shakespeare, the motive is treated both straightforwardly and indirectly (by the use of a foil), and his artistry here seems especially felicitous. Notice first that the motive of sleep is adumbrated by the connotations of Brutus's words " I have *veiled my look* " and Cassius's expression about those who " have wish'd that noble Brutus *had his eyes*." It is then introduced at the very end of the following scene with Cassius's words,

> Let us go,
> For it is after midnight, and ere day
> We will awake him and be sure of him.
>
> (I. iii. 162-4)

The word sleep is of course implied, but has not been uttered thus far. Yet the lines provide the suitable transition to the next scene which opens with the sleep motive. There is more behind the words than appears at first sight : there is a touch of irony in the fact that Cassius means to wake a man who is anything but asleep, who can no longer sleep—as we realize immediately afterwards when Brutus tries to wake his boy Lucius and exclaims " I would it were my fault to sleep so soundly." At the same time there is a play on the double meaning of the word awake : it soon appears in a figurative sense on Cassius's anonymous paper " Brutus thou sleepst : awake." And again the irony comes out— but stronger this time—when Brutus tells us a few lines further :

Since Cassius first did whet me against Caesar
I have not slept.

(II. i. 61-2)

When the conspirators are introduced in Brutus's house, moreover, and think they have awakened him, he answers : "I have
been up this hour, awake all night." Now the lack of sleep, which
Shakespeare so powerfully associates with a bad conscience in
Macbeth, he uses here to suggest the full weight of the problem
Brutus has to debate and solve ; and he makes Brutus's sleeplessness all the more effective by contrasting it to the sound sleep of
the boy Lucius. This is the main dramatic purpose of what we
might call the Lucius episodes.

These episodes are introduced with the greatest care and
provide a fine example of Shakespeare's dramatic economy. To
study them within their dramatic context, and as closely connected
elements is illuminating. To put it briefly they mark two highly
significant moments in the tragedy of Brutus, two nights of
deepest tension before a capital action : the night before the ides
of March and the night before the battle of Philippi. Each of them
leads into the dawn of decisive day, and those two days are in a
way the beginning and the end of the " work " of Brutus—as he
himself realizes when he declares with reference to Philippi :

this same day
Must end the work the ides of March begun.
(V. i. 112-3)

The Lucius episodes are thus the one recurring element which
strongly links those nights together and heightens their contrast
as the pause before the outset and the pause before the end of the
Brutus action.

Brutus calls his boy, but the boy does not answer, the boy
Lucius sleeps :

Lucius, I say!
I would it were my fault to sleep so soundly.
(II. i. 3-4)

Brutus then raises his voice and calls out louder : " When,
Lucius, when? awake, I say! what, Lucius!" This time the boy
appears : " Called you, my Lord?" He is so sleepy yet, as we
may guess, that he hasn't quite realized whether the call which
waked him was real or a dream. So sound, indeed, was his dewy-
feathered sleep. Brutus then orders him to light a taper in his

study—a sign that Brutus will remain awake. And, to be sure, the rest of the night proves of capital importance to him : he first reaches the final decision that Caesar must be killed ; he later receives the conspirators and at length discusses with them the whole plan of the action which will take place on the following morning. The weightiest matters are thus dealt with " by night, When evils are most free," and the issue involves the life of Caesar, the conspirators' own life and the fate of Rome. When " the morning comes upon " them, the conspirators leave Brutus who gives them a last inspiriting message. Then a relaxation of the tension immediately takes place. Brutus remembers his boy : " Boy! Lucius! Fast asleep!" (II. i. 229). The contrast between the soundness of the boy's sleep and the harrowing care which keeps Brutus awake is more suggestive than ever. This time Shakespeare allows Brutus himself to point it out :

> It is no matter ;
> Enjoy the honey-heavy dew of slumber :
> Thou hast no figures nor no fantasies,
> Which busy care draws in the brains of men ;
> Therefore thou sleep'st so sound.
>
> (II. i. 229-233)

At that point already the dramatic purpose of the Lucius episodes is clear : they can be considered as akin to those mirror-scenes which, in Professor Price's words, " offer some kind of contrast to the general run of the action, making it stand out more prominently by a certain difference of tone or implication."[35]

Between this and the next Lucius episode the great reversals have taken place : the conspiracy has succeeded, Caesar is fallen and Brutus brought to the pinnacle. But his triumph is brief. Antony's oration has turned the Roman people against him and Brutus fled into exile. His fortunes are now declining and he is bound to set his cause, and his life, upon one single battle. This battle is to be fought on the following day, and as night draws close, Lucius brings on tapers. For Brutus and his generals must keep an ultimate council. His own strategical plan prevails against Cassius's advice. Now " the deep of night is crept upon (their) talk," and Cassius, Messala and Titinius take leave, for nature must obey necessity which, says Brutus, " we will niggard with a little rest." Yet Brutus keeps awake, and when Lucius brings his gown he asks him for his instrument. The latter Lucius episode is now introduced with a recurrence of the sleep motive :

> What, thou speak'st drowsily?
> Poor knave, I blame thee not ; thou art o'er-watched.
> (IV. iii. 238-9)

But this time the motive gradually merges with the music theme which adds new meaning to the episode :

> Canst thou hold up thy heavy eyes awhile,
> And touch thy instrument a strain or two?
> (IV. iii. 254-5)

Clear again is the contrast between Brutus's sleeplessness and the drowsy boy who tells him " I have slept, my lord, already." The parallel with the former episode is obvious. But music and sleep, as they are now associated, are suggestive of a deeper contrast.

> This is a sleepy tune. O murderous slumber,
> Lay'st thou thy leaden mace upon my boy,
> That plays thee music? Gentle knave, good night ;
> I will not do thee so much wrong to wake thee :
> If thou dost nod, thou break'st thy instrument ;
> I'll take it from thee ; and, good boy, good night.
> (IV. iii. 265-70)

The delicacy of Brutus's feeling, who gently disengages the instrument from the sleepy boy for fear lest it should break, has often been pointed out as one of the most attractive traits in his character. But we should go beyond this. As the musical instrument is, together with the boy's sleep, a symbol of harmony, the episode as a whole gives us an imaginative epitome of Brutus's tragedy.

For his unconscious yearning for a stillness and a harmony which he has lost precisely shows in his concern for the instrument and for the child's sleep. For a brief moment it looks as if quietude and harmony were now prevailing. The delicate instrument whose tunes lulled the youthful player to sleep is saved from breaking, and Brutus kindly leaves the boy to his slumber : " I will not do thee so much wrong to wake thee." Such was Brutus's gentle purpose. With deepest irony, however, within less than twenty lines, Shakespeare has this same delicately minded Brutus shout and harshly wake up everybody : " Boy, Lucius! Varro! Claudius! Sirs, awake!" As to the instrument, the boy shaken out of his sleep but not quite out of his dream unconsciously cries out : " The strings, my lord, are false " (IV. iii. 289). There's something rotten, indeed, in Brutus's world, and the significant point is that the startling break of the spell which prompts Brutus to destroy with his calls the silent harmony he just wanted to preserve, has been brought about by the sudden apparition of Caesar's ghost.

We know then through that brief intimation why now the strings are false :

> Take but degree away, untune that string
> And, hark, what discord follows!

Thus the motive of sleep, blended with the theme of music, here imaginatively brings us back to the core of the Brutus drama. " By breaking established order . . . man, too may put all out of tune. So warned Shakespeare in *Troilus and Cressida* when Ulysses explained the inevitable order of the heavens and of state as strings of an instrument which, when altered, brings discord. When order means degree, ascent, it can no more happily be altered than can the notes of a musical scale."[36] This is precisely what Brutus is learning at his own expense. His murder of Caesar meant breaking established order, here symbolized by the harmony and stillness of sleep and music. So much, we suggest is implied in Lucius's outcry " The strings, my lord, are false."

It appears, moreover, that Brutus is the only one who saw the ghost—which is a measure of his guilt. When Lucius, now awake, tells him that he did not see anything, Brutus answers : " Sleep again, Lucius." For the last time the sleep of innocent childhood is implicitly contrasted with the restlessness that busy care draws into the brains of men. If this is the last reference to Lucius in the play, there is one more faint touch, however, of the sleep motive. And, as in more than one later play, it blends with the image of death. Just before Brutus throws himself on his sword, he visualizes the end of his " life's history " and says : " Night hangs upon my eyes." This suggests that with his death the restlessness at last is ended which began when he told Cassius " I have veiled my look," and confessed he had forgotten the shows of love to other men. With his death the cruel debt is paid, his bones can rest, night indeed will hang upon his eyes and Brutus can at last enjoy, for ever, the lulling charities of sleep.

Notes on Chapter I I

[1] G. W. Knight (*The Imperial Theme*), quoted by Stewart, *Character and Motive*, p. 49.

[2] De Quincey, quoted by Furness, *Caesar*, p. 99.

[3] *Caesar*, pp. xxvii-xxix.

[4] Stewart, *Character and Motive*, p. 52.

[5] F. Schöne, quoted by Furness, *Caesar*, pp. 25-6.

[6] Indeed, there is nothing in *King John* which can be paralleled to the dramatically important treatment of the dream motive introduced by Calpurnia's presentiments.

[7] Dover Wilson, *Hamlet* (2nd ed.), p. 146.

[8] E. E. Stoll, *Shakespeare and Other Masters*, p. 41.

[9] Professor Hemingway for one has been said to class Shakespeare " as a believer in supernaturalism " (G. C. Taylor, " Two Notes on Shakespeare ", *PQ*, XX, 1941, 371). So much indeed seems to be implied in a note of his expressing his opinion that " Shakespeare believed in Glendower's magic powers, whatever Hotspur's opinion may have been " (*New Variorum Henry IV*, ed. by S. B. Hemingway, Philadelphia, 1936, p. 201).

[10] *Character and Motive*, p. 39.

[11] On this point we may assume a quicker response on the part of the Elizabethan audience. According to Madeleine Doran, whose pertinent conclusions are worthy of notice, " The measure of the difference between the Elizabethans and us in our response to *Hamlet* is . . . that many of them would have assented to the ghost on the first level—the level of complete belief in the real world—that many would have assented to it on the second level—the level of emotional willingness to believe, however much they were in doubt rationally, and that a few would have responded to it merely on the third level, the level of purely conventional literary acceptance ; whereas we, unless we are spiritualists, respond to it entirely on this third level, or explain it away, as Dr. Greg does " (" That Undiscovered Country. A Problem concerning the Use of the Supernatural in *Hamlet* and *Macbeth*", *Renaissance Studies in Honor of Hardin Craig*, *PQ*, XX, 1941, 420).

[12] Group awareness has also been emphasized by Mr. Walter in his interesting study of Shakespeare's art in announcing ghosts, and we are bold to think that few critics would disagree with the following passage : " Presuming upon the contagion which gives the theatre its singular persuasive power, Shakespeare set about creating upon his stage the characteristic mood of people receptive to supernatural fears. When this mood communicates itself to an audience through the dependable small miracle of human sympathetic imagination, a ghost will not only be recognized for what he is, he will be heard with fear

and wonder." (H. T. Walter, "Shakspeare announces a Ghost", *S Q*, 1950, 248).

[13] On the significance of his own " conversion " to a belief in omens, see further down, pp. 42-44.

[14] *Political Characters*, p. 37.

[15] De Quincey, *op. cit.*

[16] And mark that the adjective has been literally taken over from Plutarch's " holy course ".

[17] *Political Characters*, p. 40.

[18] This he shares with his modern descendants who regularly turn to the weekly horoscopes.

[19] De Quincey, *op. cit.*

[20] That Cassius did not *fear* the elements is clear, but that he reacted to them—walking about the streets, submitting himself unto the perilous night and baring his bosom to the thunderstone—is none the less obvious. Brutus only stands aloof.

[21] Dowden, *Shakspere*, p. 292.

[22] A parallel irony might well lurk behind a scene which has baffled many a critic, and might perhaps help us to solve a vexing problem. On the stage, the simplest way out generally consists in doing away with the disturbing passage by means of a cut.

Thus, to quote but one typical instance, referring to a recent performance of *Julius Caesar* by the Masquers of Amherst College, a critic writes : " One of the cuts disposed of a problem which vexes many students of the play. The second passage mentioning the death of Portia (Messala's announcement to Brutus) was deleted, eliminating Brutus' strange pretence that he did not know of his wife's passing, although he had described it to Cassius not 40 lines earlier. This cut is conventional, and no doubt desirable " (W. A. Bacon, " *Julius Caesar* at the Folger Shakespeare Library", *Shakespeare Association Bulletin*, XXIV, 1949, 114). Now in pretending that he did not know of Portia's death, Brutus wants to show Messala that he can remain stoically immovable even when confronted with the deepest shock to his personal feelings, and thus finally *cuts a figure*—in a way *like* Caesar himself, pretending he was immovable (though, of course, in different circumstances). Is it not perhaps one aspect of the real triumph of Caesar's spirit that Brutus, his murderer, should ultimately turn like Caesar on this one point—cutting a figure of firmness (maybe the better to brace himself up against some inward apprehension) as well as on the point of superstition?

This would indeed explain why Brutus " tells a deliberate lie to Messala . . . and, what is far worse, acts the pharisee." Dover Wilson—whose words we have just quoted (*Caesar*, p. 180)—is loath to accept Brutus as acting on this point " the stoical pharisee", and favours the alternative of a textual corruption. Though plausible in itself, the assumption that we have to deal with a rejected passage which

Shakespeare omitted to delete is not only incapable of proof, but smacks of wishful thinking and is a little too handy to be entirely satisfying. Moreover, Brutus's propensity for cutting a figure of unshakable stoicism is already apparent in an immediately preceding passage, which may be said to announce the debated scene in question. At the close of the quarrel scene Brutus, for a brief moment, entirely loses his fortitude and shows surprising impatience at the poet's interference. So much so that it is the choleric Cassius who tries to soothe his sudden flash of anger :

<blockquote>Bear with him, Brutus ; 'tis his fashion.</blockquote>

<blockquote>(IV. iii. 133)</blockquote>

And a few lines further, when Cassius expresses his surprise that Brutus " could have been so angry", Brutus is again taken off his guard and acknowledges :

<blockquote>O Cassius, I am sick of many griefs.</blockquote>

<blockquote>(142)</blockquote>

Considering the tension of the quarrel scene—not to speak of other elements—such a moment of weakness is quite natural an outlet and, psychologically, entirely relevant. Yet, as soon as Brutus perceives from Cassius's casual remark,

<blockquote>Of your philosophy you make no use,
If you give place to accidental evils</blockquote>

<blockquote>(143-4)</blockquote>

that his stoical pedestal is threatened, his reaction is immediate and asserts itself in a boastful form : " No man bears sorrow better." And then he reveals the death of Portia. Nevertheless we know now that grief has sickened Brutus, that he shrinks from this momentary weakness and fights it by trying to deceive others, as well as himself, into believing that the stoical figure is still intact and stronger than ever.

This intimates how much Brutus has been undermined by his recent trials. Viewed in that light his pretence to Messala is not devoid of a pathetic element which saves him from the worse aspects of what has been called a wanton showing off. All this would seem to speak in favour of our suggested interpretation. For a different view, however, see W. D. Smith, " The Duplicate Revelation of Portia's Death", *SQ*, IV (1953), 153-161.

[23] *Caesar*, p. 193.

[24] *Ibid.*, p. 144.

[25] *Ibid.*, p. 192.

[26] *Ibid.*, p. 189.

[27] *Ibid.*, for the gap between the ideals for which the main characters stand, and their own actions, see R. A. Foakes, " An Approach to *Julius Caesar* ", *SQ*, V (1954), 259-270.

[28] The parallel is unmistakable and has already been pointed out by F. Harris (Furness, *Caesar*, p. 75) though he did not see its implications.

[29] Stewart, *Character and Motive*, p. 52.

[30] And we have not quite done yet with irony ; as Dover Wilson remarks, " Cassius, who persuades Brutus to kill Caesar, also persuades him to kill himself " (*Caesar*, p. 189). Is it a coincidence that he should have been so successful there, whereas his sound advice was spontaneously, almost systematically, rejected by Brutus?

[31] A. Sewell, *Character and Society in Shakespeare*, Oxford (1951), p. 56.

[32] That eminently " royalist " simile is not devoid of a particular flavour in the stern Republican's mouth. So is Brutus's unconscious recognition of the importance of leadership in his rejection of Cassius's proposal to let Antony fall together with Caesar :

> For he can do no more than Caesar's arm
> When Caesar's head is off.
>
> (II. i. 182-3)

[33] Curiously enough Sir Mark Hunter refuses to see any irony " in all this " (*Politics and Character*, 126). As soon, however, as the interplay of Shakespearean irony is studied structurally, its role becomes more and more pervasive—and here we cannot but fully endorse Professor Price's penetrating comments on " Shakespeare's never-sleeping irony " (*Construction*, 22).

[34] E. E. Stoll, "A German Producer's *Hamlet* ", *SQ*, I (1950), 40.

[35] H. T. Price, " Mirror-Scenes in Shakespeare ", *John Quincey Adams Memorial Studies*, The Folger Shakespeare Library, Washington (1948), p. 102.

[36] See Gretchen L. Finney's recent and stimulating article entitled "A World of Instruments ", *ELH*, XX (1953), 87-120. The passage here quoted is from p. 103.

STRUCTURAL IMAGERY

Imagery is a subject which has attracted many recent Shakespearian critics from Spurgeon and Knight to Clemen and
Heilman, and the word is used in more than one sense. Following
Mr. Bethell in one of his recent articles, we shall here " widen
the scope of the term ' image ' to cover any reference in word or
phrase to a distinct object or class of objects, whether used
figuratively or directly."[1] In that broader sense imagery also
includes iterative words, the recurrence of which so often enhances
the unity of a group of scenes.[2] Now iterative words, or sets
of words, often transcend their purely contextual uses, and when
over and above their immediate textual purpose they further
harp upon one of the very keynotes in the central theme of the
play, we have indeed to deal with a kind of imagery which may
be called structural. Let us take an illustration.

Typical in *Julius Caesar*—as has often been pointed out—is animal
imagery. It occurs, for instance, in connection with Caesar's death.
In his attempt to " purify the violent act of all taint of butchery
and raise it to the level of sacrifice,"[3] Brutus opposes the ritual
killing of an animal offered as a holocaust to the gods, to the
hunters' massacre of a wild beast left as a prey to the dogs :

> Let's carve him as a dish fit for the gods,
> Not hew him as a carcass fit for hounds.
>
> (II. i. 173-4)

Caesar is compared to a sacrificial victim, a noble prey who must
be dealt with nobly. Imagery vividly helps to convey Brutus's
endeavour to avoid even the faintest smack of butchery by turning
the murderer's weapon in his hand into the high priest's knife.
But if such is its immediate textual value, the imagery here is also
used with wider implications and reaches to a striking parallel
beyond the present passage. In a later scene, the same kind of
imagery is indeed taken over again with reference to Caesar's
murder, but by Antony this time, and with quite opposite connotations. Addressing Caesar's bleeding corpse in front of the
conspirators, Antony cries out :

> Here wast thou bay'd, brave hart ;
> Here didst thou fall, and here thy hunters stand,

Sign'd in thy spoil and crimson'd in thy lethe.
(III. i. 205-7)

The recurrence of the hunting imagery is significant. Though Antony did not know of Brutus's pretence to confer dignity on the murder by having it appear as a rite, ironically enough he compares Caesar to the hunters' victim, thus tacitly reducing the act to the level of sport—i.e., unnecessary and wanton killing—precisely what Brutus so much wanted to avoid. Furthermore, a hart at bay suggests a noble prey surrounded not only by hunters, who may be princes, but—what Antony cautiously leaves out of the picture—by a pack of dogs. And if we carry the associational links implicit in the picture to their natural limit, we meet with Brutus's rejected image—what is left of a hart after a kill is of course no other than " a carcass fit for hounds!"

But Antony needs not be tacit very long. As soon as he is left alone, the fateful word bursts out of his lips : " butchers!" A far cry, indeed, from sacerdotal dignity wielding the sacrificial knife. The recurrent imagery thus provides a powerful link between the two passages, and this link of course enhances their dramatic effect : the stark opposition between Brutus's and Antony's attitudes towards the murder of Caesar (one of the antithetical elements in the play) is thus vividly intimated. In that sense the imagery linking the two scenes may be considered as structural. But on the whole it is not primarily structural. In the latter passage we have quoted, however—and this is perhaps no mere chance—we meet with further imagery which is essentially structural : " Here didst thou *fall*, and here thy hunters *stand*." The powerful antithesis between " stand " and " fall," as we shall see, indeed provides the one predominant type of imagery in the play and has been most brilliantly worked out.

At the outset of the play, Caesar stands high—much too high in fact for not being a challenge to those opposite forces who want to bring him down. Shortly after his fall Brutus in his turn stands high—but we know that he is also doomed to fall. And thus, two " mighty opposites " are in turn destined to stand high and then to lie, and from the fall of one hero to the fall of the other, the play majestically sweeps. The imagery centred on the antithesis between " rise " or " stand," on the one side, and " fall " or " lie ", on the other, is so crucial, and its bearing on the main theme so obvious, that it hardly needs emphasis. In fact, when trying to put it into focus, we shall not run too great a risk " to court every sort of freak interpretation."[4] But what is less obvious is the extent, and subtlety, of its elaboration within the drama. And this well repays careful scrutiny.

*   *   *

Judging from the many passages which refer to it in Shakespeare's plays,[5] Caesar's fall seems to have had as many reverberations in the dramatist's mind as has the one hundred letters long compound "cataracting", as it were, the thundering pftjschute of Finnegan. No wonder if the image of this fall should loom so large in the very tragedy of which Caesar is the titular hero :
    O what a fall was there, my countrymen!
Thus is the echo of this fall heard again more than once after Caesar has been struck down, uttering his dying words " Et tu, Brute? Then fall Caesar!"

Our first object will be to examine the images reverberating the tragic fall just after Caesar's murder. But if we have a certain number of echoes of the fall after it has taken place, we have also a remarkable series of anticipatory hints, fraught with dramatic irony, all foreshadowing that tremendous event. Indeed, the images premonitory of the fall are worked out in so elaborate and subtle a gradation that they well deserve a close examination. At the same time we shall endeavour to keep aware of the reality of stage effect which is so easily, and dangerously, forgotten once we have been ensnared by the magic of poetic imagery.

Echoes of the Fall.

A first instance of the deliberate and often repeated contrast between " fall " and " stand " immediately follows the murder of Caesar. This contrast may be easily overlooked since " stand " is not directly opposed to " fall " within the same period, but appears a few lines further and is used quite naturally in its own different context. The word, however, occurs no less than three times within eight lines ;[6] and in view of the later development of the antithetical imagery, how can we doubt that it is a first delicate announcement of the contrast so explicit and effective in the line we have already quoted from Antony's speech :
    Here didst thou *fall*, and here thy hunters *stand*.
Though, as we said, the antithetical words are not at first directly opposed to each other within the same immediate sense-unit, the mere fact of their being used in such a proximity, more or less unconsciously prepares the mind for a closer juxtaposition. So that when they do finally appear in the same breath, as it were,

the effect is all the more striking because they have already come within reach of each other, like particles with opposite charges gradually drawing closer and meeting at last in the final flash.

There is a fourth appearance of the word " stand " about ten lines further, but this time rather than glancing back at the preceding "fall", it announces a new group of contrasting images :

> That we shall die, we know ; 'tis but the time,
> And drawing days out, that men *stand upon*.
> (III. i. 110-1)

This term is ultimately opposed to " lies along " in the famous lines :

> How many times shall Caesar bleed in sport,
> That now on Pompey's basis *lies along*
> No worthier than the dust!
> (III. i. 115-17)

But between the two opposites we have further imagery subtly hinting at upwards and downwards movements. The thrice repeated " stoop ":

> *Stoop*, Romans, *stoop*,
> And let us bathe our hands in Caesar's blood
> (III. i. 106-7)

and " *Stoop* then, and wash " (112) is indeed contrasted to the reverse motion in the line " waving our red weapons *o'er our heads* " (110). Following Armstrong,[7] we may even read, by sound echo, the word " base " in " Pompey's *basis*," and this " base " would of course be the counterpart of " lofty " in " this our *lofty* scene!"[8]

To those who might be inclined to think this somewhat far-fetched, we shall answer that as all these contrasting words (ultimately implying the same set of antithetical imagery) occur within sixteen lines only, such contrasts are not likely to be accidental.[9]

The next set of imagery connected with the fall follows very close upon this,[10] and its ironical references have already been pointed out by Brents Stirling.[11] On the one hand it glances back at Brutus's "sacrificial mood", with the strong emphasis on prostration as if, indeed, before a high priest :

> Thus, Brutus, did my master bid me *kneel* ;
> Thus did Mark Antony bid me *fall down* ;

And, *being prostrate*, thus he bade me say.

(III. i. 124-26)

It provides at the same time a new reference to "lie": "How Caesar hath deserved *to lie* in death" (133). The accumulation of the terms here in such a close succession certainly reaches beyond their immediate textual use. On the other hand, the group subtly foreshadows Antony's own development of the antithetical imagery which reaches a first peak in the simile of the hunters standing in front of the fallen hart, "crimsoned" in its blood, and rises to its vengeful climax towards the end of the great funeral oration. For as soon as he appears, the very first words he speaks are addressed to Caesar's body—though he ought to have first answered Brutus's welcome—and they strike up the keynote of the theme:

O mighty Caesar! dost thou *lie so low*?
Are all thy conquests, glories, triumphs, spoils,
Shrunk to this little measure?

(III. i. 149-51)

There is a moving element in the contrast independent of the circumstances of Caesar's death: the past splendour of a great conqueror adds poignancy to his sudden death, and "the noble dust of Alexander" more eloquently expresses than a beggar's the nothingness of man in death. And thus, what sight could be more awe-inspiring than

Imperious Caesar, dead and turn'd to clay!

In the hunting simile, moreover, there is a shift in the emotional emphasis: the light is no longer focussed on Caesar only but takes in the murderers as well in the same flash. And the scene calls forth further pity by the mere contrast between one brave and single victim bayed and killed by several hunters:

How like a deer strucken by many princes
Dost thou here *lie!*

Growing deeper and deeper, this pity it is which finally turns the "many princes" into the ironical

honourable men
Whose daggers have stabbed Caesar,

to give the angry crowd its cue: traitors, villains and murderers! From this first peak the antithetical imagery recedes until it reaches its grand climax in Antony's oration. But it does not entirely vanish. A few faint touches are scattered and are in themselves reminiscences enough to provide subjacent links. First there is Cassius's aside " I know not what may *fall* " (244). Then Antony's prophecy :

> *Over* thy wounds now do I prophesy . . .
> A curse shall *light upon* the limbs of men,
> (260, 263)

which ends in an opposition between " hot from *hell* " and " *above the earth* " (272, 275). Further, when Octavius Caesar's servant arrives and delivers his message to Antony, he suddenly sees the bleeding body and stops in the middle of a sentence to weep and, unobtrusively enough, there comes again the " stand-lie " opposition. Passion, says Antony, is catching

> for mine eyes,
> Seeing those beads of sorrow *stand* in thine,
> Began to water. Is thy master coming?
> *Serv.*   He *lies* to-night within seven leagues of Rome.
> (284-87)

Though indirectly expressed, the recurrence of the key contrast is hardly fortuitous.

Finally, some slight hints occur in Brutus's oration. In the words of the third Plebeian, " The noble Brutus is *ascended* " and now in the course of his address, Brutus explains why he " *rose* against Caesar," and then rhetorically asks :

> Who is there so *base* that would be a bondman?
> (III. ii. 11, 21, 28)

But let us now turn to the climax. It does not come abruptly, but in a fine ebb and flow. Antony has delivered the first part of his oration and he pauses to weep. This brief pause is used to show the first reactions of the plebeians, and it is clear that they are already shaken by Antony's words. Now Antony begins again to speak, and the key contrast reappears as directly as it did in the hunting image :

> But yesterday the word of Caesar might
> Have *stood* against the world : now *lies* he there,
> And none so poor to do him reverence.
> (III. ii. 119-21)

What makes the antithetical imagery here more effective—and this cannot be too strongly emphasized—is its scenic relevance. All the time, we must remember, we have before us the vision of the forcible contrast between Caesar, lying at Pompey's "basis," and the figure of Pompey himself, standing on its pedestal, and such vision makes us more keenly perceptive of the recurrence of the "stand-lie" imagery. Poetic vision and scenic effect thus coalesce, and this at the most significant moment in the drama.

Following the key contrast, a few references to downward movements may be mentioned. Should the people but hear of Caesar's testament, says Antony,

> they would go and kiss dead Caesar's wounds
> And *dip* their napkins in his sacred blood.
>
> (III. ii. 132-33)

This glances back at (and is effective counter-ritual to) Brutus's own blood rite :

> Stoop, Romans, stoop
> And let us bathe our hands in Caesar's blood
> Up to the elbows, and besmear our swords.
>
> (III. i. 106-8)

Furthermore, within less than ten lines, we have a threefold reference to Antony's coming down from the pulpit to show the people " him that made the will "—

> Shall I *descend*? and will you give me leave?
>
> All.   *Come down*
> Sec. Cit. *Descend*—

opposed to the iterative word " stand " which immediately follows and is repeated no less than five times :

> Fourth Cit. A ring ; *stand* round.
> First Cit.   *Stand* from the hearse, *stand* from the
>   body. . . .
> Ant.   Nay, press not so upon me ; *stand* far
>   off.
> All.   *Stand* back.
>
> (III. ii. 160-68)

In view of the visual contrast between the plebeians standing in a ring about the corpse of Caesar and the inanimate body lying on the ground, the imagery is again closely related to scenic effect.

Now Antony can afford to attack the murderers directly. His emphasis on the cruel aspect of the assassination culminates in the description of Caesar's moving death—with the *coup de grâce* of Brutus's stab. Antithetical imagery then finds its most vigorous expression with the great evocation of the fall—a fall of such magnitude that it transcends the individual character of Caesar to take on vast collective significance :

> then burst his mighty heart ;
> And, in his mantle muffling up his face,
> Even at the base of Pompey's statue,
> Which all the while ran blood, great Caesar fell.
> O, what a fall was there, my countrymen!
> Then I, and you, and all of us fell down,
> Whilst bloody treason flourish'd over us.
> (III. ii. 186-92)

All those who are honest and loyal are, as it were, tumbling down together with Caesar, while traitors only stand and flourish over the scene. This is a culminating point ; at that juncture the fall reverberates in the heart of every man in the audience—a most ominous echo for the murderers—and when the body is uncovered, passion gushes out with tumultuous force and rises in a blind and furious flood against the conspirators. It is the last great flash of antithetical imagery. A total reversal in the fortunes of the opposite parties has taken place, and those hunters who stood around the hart to sound the mort are now inexorably driven to bay.

The play ends with a last brief funeral touch : for if Antony finally comes to praise Brutus, not to bury him, Octavius Caesar it is who takes care of the body :

> Within my tent his bones to-night shall lie.

It is perhaps no chance occurrence that one of the very last words concerning Brutus—in the last sentence but one of the final scene—should be the world "lie". There is a tide indeed in the affairs of men.

*   *   *

Foreshadowings of the Fall

When he set about to present the death of Caesar on the scene, Shakespeare knew that he could rely on even the lowest illiterate among the groundlings knowing that his hero fell a victim under

F

the knife of conspirators. He could thus play most skilfully on dramatic irony and dramatic audience, and scored perhaps the finest effects by means of the " stand and lie—rise and fall " images, such converging images being as many subtle pre-figurations of Caesar's real fall.

The imagery is deliberately concentrated on some given points to heighten dramatic effect, the first part of the scene leading to the murder being, of course, the most obvious case of all. But if cumulative effect makes the foreshadowing imagery more striking in this passage, prefigurations of the fall are clear enough in at least two preceding scenes. It is in connection with Casca's account of the offering of the crown to Caesar that the imagery premonitory of the fall first flares up.

Casca is garrulous enough not to make the remarkable iteration of the preterite " fell " seem unnatural. We must realize, however, that it is repeated no less than five times within twenty lines : " he swounded and *fell down* at it (I. ii. 247). . . . He *fell down* in the market-place (251). . . . I am sure Caesar *fell down* (256-7). . . . Marry, before he *fell down* (262). . . . And so he *fell*" (267). For the audience, who know all the time that Caesar is soon to fall— not in a swoon but under the cursed steel of the murderers, is this bell-like repetition not felt as a sort of ironically foreshadowing knell? And this all the more since Brutus's interruption " he hath the falling-sickness," adds fine dramatic irony to the passage : Cassius shows himself sensitive to its hidden meaning—though not in the same sense, of course, as the audience—when he remarks : " No, Caesar hath it not : but you, and I, And honest Casca, we have the falling-sickness " (254-5). What he implicitly means is that Caesar has grown so great because honest people are falling low—as he has just said before : " The fault . . . is . . . in ourselves, that we are underlings " (I. ii. 140-1). Perhaps Shakespeare remembered this passage as he was writing Antony's lines telling the people that when great Caesar fell, " Then, I, and you, and all of us fell down " (III. ii. 191).

Apart from the passage preceding the murder itself, antithetical imagery is also clustered in the scene of the conspirators' meeting at Brutus's house. The scene, we remember, begins with Brutus's soliloquy, and there we already have an introductory touch :

> But 'tis a common proof,
> That *lowliness* is young ambition's ladder,
> Whereto the *climber-upward* turns his face ;

> But when he once attains the *upmost* round,
> He then unto the ladder turns his back,
> Looks in *the clouds*, scorning the *base degrees*
> By which he did *ascend*.
>
> (II. i. 21-27)

The phrase " looks in the clouds " harps again on the challenge of Caesar's greatness and should be linked—through Cassius's wondering " That he is grown so great " (I. ii. 150)—with Flavius's striking image of a birdlike Caesar who " would soar above the view of men " (I. i. 75). Now all those who are intent on having him fly an ordinary pitch are assembled, and though it is yet dark the rising sun is referred to—another image of greatness :

> Here, as I point my sword, the sun *arises* ;
> Which is a great way *growing* on the south, . . .
> Some two months hence *up higher* toward the north
> He first presents his fire, and the *high* east
> *Stands* as the Capitol, directly here.
>
> (II. i. 106-11)

The juxtaposition of the high east with the Capitol is significant : that towering height will make the coming fall, which keeps pressing on our minds, more shattering ; and, in fact, the lofty image has hardly vanished than the fateful tumble is again suggested :

> So let *high*-sighted tyranny range on
> Till each man *drop* by lottery.
>
> (118-19)

A fall is inescapable : *we* know who is to fall and who is to rise, the characters don't as yet (and part of the thrill and suspense of the dramatic audience we cannot but share) ; but one thing they know for certain : " this shall be or we will *fall* for it " (II. i. 128). Their resolve is inflexible and finds its noblest expression in Brutus's phrase (when refusing Cassius's proposal to " let Antony and Caesar *fall* together ") :

> We all *stand up* against the spirit of Caesar.
>
> (II. i. 167)

After this new iteration of the key contrast between " stand " and "fall", antithetical imagery vanishes for some time. When it emerges again it closely precedes, and leads to, Caesar's death :

> Casca, you are the first that *rears* your hand.
>
> (III.i. 30)

With this word everything is ready and the course of events runs according to scheme. Metellus kneels and addresses " most high " Caesar, who scornfully waves aside

> These *couchings* and these *lowly* courtesies . . .
> *Low*-crooked court'sies and *base* spaniel-fawning.
>
> (III. i. 36,43)

Yet Cassius not only chimes in but outdoes Metellus :

> As *low* as to thy foot doth Cassius *fall*.
>
> (56)

And now, as a supreme dramatic irony, the Caesar who is already encircled by armed conspirators about to strike at him, who is about to be hurled down from his dizzy pedestal into piteous death and dust, makes his profession of constancy as if his position were so high and so secure as to be unassailable :

> I am constant as the northern star,
> Of whose true-fix'd and resting quality
> There is no fellow in the firmament.
> . . . there's but one in all doth hold his place . . . but one
> That unassailable holds on his rank,
> Unshaked of motion.
>
> (60-70)

In fact, within the same minute Olympus is not only lifted up, but so violent and irresistible is the sudden commotion that it crumbles in a shattering downfall—unshaked of motion, indeed!

Now that we more fully visualize to what extent the antithetical imagery has been artistically worked out to fit the very sweep of the whole drama, we may perhaps conclude our brief survey by reverting to the first scene in the play with some new awareness as to its structural aspect.

The relevance of this introductory scene to the rest of the play has often been pointed out, and some critics have expatiated on the capital part played by the one collective character in the drama, the Roman crowd. Its relevance, however, goes deeper perhaps than has been commonly realized, for there already we have the first flashes of antithetical imagery as a prelude to the greater fireworks.

As soon as Shakespeare breaks into verse, we have the key contrast between "high" and "low". Many a time and oft, says Marullus to the commoners,

> Have you *climb'd up* to walls and battlements,
> To *towers* and windows, yea, to chimney-*tops* . . .
> To see *great* Pompey pass the streets of Rome,

and so great was the universal shout

> That Tiber trembled *underneath* her banks
> To hear the replication of your sounds
> Made in her *concave* shores.
>   (I. i. 38-48)

The contrast is deliberate, and it is unwittingly taken over again by Flavius—with the greater impact of the superlatives—when he enjoins the commoners to weep into the Tiber

> till the *lowest* stream
> Do kiss the *most exalted* shores of all.
>   (60-1)

A powerful image which announces in a way the greater disturbance of the elements, when the ocean rises to be " exalted with the threat'ning clouds " and the tempest is dropping fire.

Finally, as we have seen, the speech ends with the first statement —in a brilliant flight image—of the challenge of Caesar's greatness.

                        *   *   *

Brief and incomplete as it is, this study of the structural imagery may perhaps help in revealing to what extent the drama has been wrought into an organic whole. The entire structure of the play viewed globally as well as in its minute constituents really forms a living body with flesh, and blood, and spirit marvellously commingled.

If so many riches are stored in a relatively simple play like *Julius Caesar* as soon as we are to examine its structure, what treasures shall we find in the structure of a play like *Hamlet*?

When in a famous passage a poet applied (or rather, to borrow his own phrasing, reclaimed for our dramatist) the term " myriad-minded ", he made perhaps one of the best shots towards solving the ultimate mystery of the Shakespeare phenomenon. For it is a mystery which partakes of the infinite—and, so far, the infinite has always remained unfathomable.

Notes on Chapter III

[1] S. L. Bethell, " Shakespeare's Imagery : The diabolic Images in *Othello* ", *Sh. Survey*, V (1952), 62.

[2] See R. A. Foakes, " Suggestions for a new Approach to Shakespeare's Imagery ", *Sh. Survey*, V (1952), 81, 91.

[3] Brents Stirling, *op. cit. (PMLA)*, 769.

[4] Mr. Bethell's caveat, *op. cit.*, 65.

[5] Cf. D. S. Brewer, " Brutus' Crime : A Footnote to *Julius Caesar* ", *RES*, III N.S. (1952), 51-54.

[6] " *stand* still " (III. i. 83), " *Stand* fast together " (88), " Talk not of *standing* " (90).

[7] See E. A. Armstrong, *Shakespeare's Imagination. A Study of the Psychology of Association and Inspiration*, London (1946).

[8] The word " base " is also in Plutarch, though used a little earlier than in Shakespeare. But " lofty " is new and so the contrast deliberately introduced. Moreover, Pompey's " base " occurs in Antony's oration. See below, pp. 67-68.

[9] Pompey's basis is richer in implications than might appear at first sight. There is an interesting point here which is worth noting. Plutarch makes the most of the coincidence that Caesar died at the foot of Pompey's statue, pointing out that it looked like a sort of posthumous vengeance : " Caesar was driven either casually or purposedly, by the council of conspirators, against the base whereupon Pompey's image stood, which ran all of a gore-blood till he was slain. Thus it seemed that the image took *just revenge* of Pompey's enemy, being thrown down on the ground at his feet, and yielding up his ghost there, for the number of wounds he had upon him." It is remarkable that, provided with so salient a feature, Shakespeare entirely dropped the revenge motive, or left it so subjacent that it passes practically unnoticed. This is not difficult to explain. We must remember that from now on the prevailing sentiment towards Caesar must be one of pity for the murdered man as a human being, and that this pity must not be allayed by so clear a suggestion that Caesar's blood is flowing as if in revenge (and, following Plutarch's words, a " just revenge " at that) for Pompey's blood.

But one thing Shakespeare did not want to drop was the " stand-lie " connotation lurking behind this dramatically effective traditional trait. The connotation carries with it the idea of the wheel of Fortune, precipitating the one who stood high and elevating the other but to bring him down again. This may well be the first hint that a time will come when he who calls the murder a lofty scene, and stands so high over Caesar's blood (" Brutus shall lead, and we will grace his heels " (121) will also lie so low, " no worthier than the dust." (And why " dust " if not because—apart from its obvious Biblical connotations—it also suggests something that lies under our feet? Is there not perhaps the same suggestion in Antony's corresponding expression " bleeding piece of earth "?) Just as he who came in triumph over Pompey's blood and bestrode the world like a Colossus (mark the image of a gigantic statue which is also implied here) now lies so low, all his glories shrunk to this little measure! Shakespeare could rely on the hidden power of such associations because that part of Roman history was common knowledge.

[10] The word referring to Brutus's leadership " we will *grace his heels* " providing the link.

[11] " Here a threefold repetition, ' kneel ', ' fall down ', and ' being prostrate ', brings the ceremonial irony close to a level of satire " (*op. cit. PMLA*, 770).

BIBLIOGRAPHY

This bibliography is strictly limited to the works quoted, or referred to, in the present study

E. A. ARMSTRONG, *Shakespeare's Imagination. A Study of the Psychology of Association and Inspiration*, London (1946).

W. A. BACON, "*Julius Caesar* at the Folger Shakespeare Library", *Shakespeare Association Bulletin*, XXIV (1949).

S. L. BETHELL, "Shakespeare's Imagery : The diabolic Images in *Othello*", *Shakespeare Survey*, V (1952).

D. S. BREWER, "Brutus' Crime : A Footnote to *Julius Caesar*", *Review of English Studies*, III N.S. (1952).

B. R. BREYER, "A New Look at *Julius Caesar*", *Essays in Honor of Walter Clyde Curry*, Nashville (1954).

L. B. CAMPBELL, "Political Ideas in *Macbeth*, IV, iii," *Shakespeare Quarterly*, II (1951).

O. J. CAMPBELL, "The Salvation of Lear", *English Literary History*, XV (1948).

H. B. CHARLTON, *Shakespearian Tragedy*, Cambridge (1948).

J. V. CUNNINGHAM, "'Tragedy' in Shakespeare", *English Literary History*, XVII (1950).

M. DORAN, "That Undiscovered Country. A Problem concerning the Use of the Supernatural in *Hamlet* and *Macbeth*", *Renaissance Studies in Honor of Hardin Craig, Philological Quarterly*, XX (1941).

T. S. DORSCH, ed., *Julius Caesar*, Revised Arden Shakespeare, London (1955).

E. DOWDEN, *Shakspere : His Mind and Art*, 13 ed., London (1906).

A. F. FAIRCHILD, *Shakespeare and the Tragic Theme*, Columbia (1944).

M. FELHEIM, "The Problem of Time in *Julius Caesar*", *Huntington Library Quarterly*, XIII (1950).

G. L. FINNEY, "A World of Instruments", *English Literary History*, XX (1953).

R. A. FOAKES, "Suggestions for a new Approach to Shakespeare's Imagery", *Shakespeare Survey*, V (1952).

R. A. FOAKES, "An Approach to *Julius Caesar*", *Shakespeare Quarterly*, V (1954).

H. H. FURNESS, Jr., ed., *Julius Caesar*, New Variorum Shakespeare, Philadelphia (1913).

A. HARBAGE, *As They Liked It. An Essay on Shakespeare and Morality*, New York (1947).

S. B. HEMINGWAY, ed., *Henry IV*, New Variorum Shakespeare, Philadelphia (1936).

M. HUNTER, "Politics and Character in Shakespeare's 'Julius Caesar'", *Essays by Divers Hands*, X, London (1931).

G. W. KNIGHT, *The Imperial Theme*, Oxford (1951 edn.).

L. C. KNIGHTS, "Shakespeare and Political Wisdom", *Sewanee Review*, LXI (1953).

M. W. MACCALLUM, *Shakespeare's Roman Plays and their Background*, London (1910).

L. MORSBACH, "Shakespeare's Cäsarbild", *Studien zur Englischen Philologie*, LXXXVIII, Halle (1935).

R. G. MOULTON, *Shakespeare as a Dramatic Artist*, 3 ed., Oxford (1906).

K. MUIR, ed., *Macbeth*, Revised Arden Shakespeare, London (1951).

J. PALMER, *Political Characters of Shakespeare*, London (1945).

J. E. PHILLIPS, *The State in Shakespeare's Greek and Roman Plays*, New York (1940).

H. T. PRICE, "Mirror-Scenes in Shakespeare", *John Quincey Adams Memorial Studies*, Washington (1948).

H. T. PRICE, "Construction in Shakespeare", *University of Michigan Contributions in Modern Philology*, No. 17 (1951).

M. E. PRIOR, *The Language of Tragedy*, New York (1947).

E. SCHANZER, "The Tragedy of Shakespeare's Brutus", *English Literary History*, XXII (1955).

A. SEWELL, *Character and Society in Shakespeare*, Oxford (1951).

W. D. SMITH, "The Duplicate Revelation of Portia's Death", *Shakespeare Quarterly*, IV (1953).

D. A. STAUFFER, *Shakespeare's World of Images*, New York (1949).

J. I. M. STEWART, *Character and Motive in Shakespeare*, London (1949).

B. STIRLING, *The Populace in Shakespeare*, New York (1949).

B. STIRLING, "Or Else This Were a Savage Spectacle", *Publications of the Modern Language Association of America*, LXVI (1951).

E. E. STOLL, *Shakespeare and Other Masters*, Cambridge Mass. (1940).

E. E. STOLL, "A German Producer's *Hamlet*", *Shakespeare Quarterly*, I (1950).

G. C. TAYLOR, "Two Notes on Shakespeare", *Philological Quarterly*, XX (1941).

E. M. W. TILLYARD, *Shakespeare's History Plays*, 3 imp., London (1951).

R. WALKER, "The Northern Star: An Essay on the Roman Plays", *Shakespeare Quarterly*, II (1951).

H. T. WALTER, "Shakespeare announces a Ghost", *Shakespeare Quarterly*, I (1950).

M. WICKERT, "Antikes Gedankengut in Shakespeares Julius Cäsar", *Shakespeare Jahrbuch*, Bd. 82/83 (1948).

J. D. WILSON, ed., *Hamlet*, 2nd edn., Cambridge (1936).

J. D. WILSON, ed., *Julius Caesar*, Cambridge (1949).

INDEX